BATIKS AND BEYOND

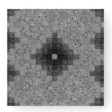

BATIKS AND

LAURIE J. SHIFRIN

BEYOND
QUILTS FROM FABULOUS FABRICS

Martingale®
& COMPANY

Credits

PRESIDENT • *Nancy J. Martin*
CEO • *Daniel J. Martin*
PUBLISHER • *Jane Hamada*
EDITORIAL DIRECTOR • *Mary V. Green*
MANAGING EDITOR • *Tina Cook*
TECHNICAL EDITOR • *Laurie Baker*
COPY EDITOR • *Ellen Balstad*
DESIGN DIRECTOR • *Stan Green*
ILLUSTRATOR • *Laurel Strand*
TEXT DESIGNER • *Trina Stahl*
COVER DESIGNER • *Stan Green*
PHOTOGRAPHER • *Brent Kane*

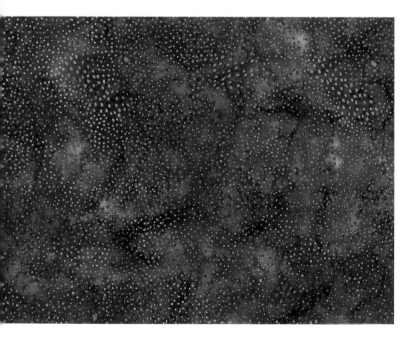

Mission Statement

*Dedicated to providing quality products and service
to inspire creativity.*

That Patchwork Place® is an imprint of
Martingale & Company®.

Batiks and Beyond: Quilts from Fabulous Fabrics
© 2003 by Laurie J. Shifrin

Martingale & Company
20205 144th Avenue NE
Woodinville, WA 98072-8478 USA
www.martingale-pub.com

Printed in the USA
08 07 06 05 04 03   8 7 6 5 4 3 2 1

Library of Congress Cataloging-in-Publication Data
Shifrin, Laurie J.
  Batiks and beyond : quilts from fabulous fabrics /
Laurie J. Shifrin.
    p. cm.
Includes bibliographical references and index.
  ISBN 1-56477-470-8
 1. Patchwork—Patterns. 2. Quilting—Patterns.
3. Appliqué—Patterns. 4. Batik. I. Title
  TT835S4654 2003
  746 . 46 ' 041—dc21
                                        2003008956

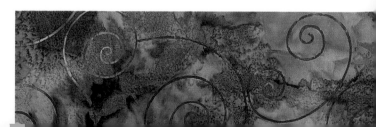

Dedication

I DEDICATE this book to my wonderful friend Carol Boyer for her never-ending support. Though she won't take credit for her contributions, this book (as well as the last) would never have materialized without her help.

Acknowledgments

MANY THANKS go to the following people:
Sharon and Jason Yenter, who have been supportive throughout the publication of my first book as well as the writing of this, my second. They are unendingly generous with their encouragement and understanding;
Trish Carey, Diane Roubal, Margy Duncan, Kara Smith, and Sue Gross for their help with bindings;
Janine Jijina for her creative input and support; and
the wonderful staff of Martingale & Company, especially Laurie Baker, my editor, for their dedication to producing beautiful, informative, and inspiring quilt books.

I extend special thanks to Hoffman California International Fabrics; Princess Mirah/Bali Fabrications; Valori Wells; Kona Bay Fabrics; Marcus Brothers; Trans-Pacific Textiles, Ltd.; Island Batiks; In The Beginning Fabrics; Judy Robertson; Log Cabin Hand-Dyed Fabrics; and Bold Over Batiks! for designing and then supplying me with many of the incredible fabrics you see in this book.

CONTENTS

INTRODUCTION

IT IS SO exciting for me to see the growing popularity of batiks in quilts. One of the true joys of teaching patterns from my first book, *Batik Beauties* (Martingale & Company, 2001), is the feeling of gratification I receive when I see a quilter delve into the beautiful colors and unusual patterns of batiks for the first time and produce a stunning quilt. For me, batiks have never lost their allure, so much so that I can't wait to see the bold designs and magnificent colors in each new batch of batiks that arrive at the quilt shop where I work. At each Quilt Market, where fabric companies introduce their latest fabric lines, I see more and more companies venturing into the batik world, thus increasing the variety of batik styles available to quilters.

I wanted this book, like *Batik Beauties*, to offer unique quilt patterns that focus on the use of batiks. However, I also wanted to show the versatility of the patterns and batiks. To achieve these goals, I give instructions for eleven quilts made entirely of batiks. Each project comes with yardage and cutting instructions for multiple sizes as well as a photograph of a quilt made in a different size and/or fabric combination from the featured project. Sometimes this alternate version is done in a new batik color group, sometimes it uses a combination of batiks and nonbatiks, and sometimes it is made completely with nonbatiks. Note that listed fabric requirements and illustrations reflect the main batik project.

I hope that by including variations of my quilts, I will encourage quilters to see beyond my color schemes. We all know that one color scheme doesn't suit everyone; patterns can be made in almost any color combination. By providing a few views and different size options, I hope that quilters will adapt the patterns to fit their size and color needs.

How borders affect the overall appearance of a quilt is intriguing to me. We can move away from the traditional frame border and on to more imaginative ways to complete a quilt top. For the projects in this book, I have created borders that are part of the *design* of the quilts and that affect the impact of the quilts, often in a subtle way. I hope you'll try these borders on other future quilt projects.

Each one of the quilts in this book is meant for quilters with some quilting experience. The shapes used are simple; mostly squares, rectangles, and triangles. None of the quilts are very difficult, but due to the need for precise piecing, I would not consider any of them beginner-level projects. I recommend "Mixed Up but Not Crazy" (page 54) and "Pineapple Princess" (page 23) as two of the simpler designs. For patterns that are slightly more complicated, move on to "Spice Market" (page 16), "Twinkle Toes" (page 75), and "Patchwork Puzzle" (page 88). "Arboretum in Autumn" (page 66) is an even more intricate pattern, but give it a try and you'll see it only requires careful cutting and pressing.

BATIK BASICS

In the following sections, I include information about batiks—their weave, dyes, and fabric preparation—as well as advice for choosing fabrics for your project. You can find instructions on basic quiltmaking techniques after the projects, beginning on page 96.

RIGHT SIDE OR WRONG SIDE?

In the batik-making process, wax is applied to plain fabric in a desired design before colored dyes are applied. The wax sinks into the fabric, resulting in a clear image on both sides of the fabric after the dyes are applied. Occasionally, there is an obvious right and wrong side to the fabric, but more often than not, it is hard to distinguish between the two. If the sides are virtually identical, I usually choose the side on which the design is clearer and has less-fuzzy edges. If the colors vary from side to side, I choose the side with the color that suits a particular project best.

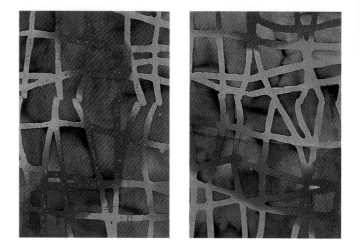

The areas on the fabric at left show spotted areas where the wax did not saturate the fabric; this is the wrong side. The clearer design at right is the fabric's right side.

This batik has different coloring on each side, so you can use whichever side best suits your project.

This fabric has a definite right (left) and wrong (right) side.

WEAVE

THE THREAD count of fabrics commonly used for quilting ranges from the tight weave of pima and lawn to medium-weave poplin and loose-weave sheeting. Batiks are usually made from fabrics at the tighter end of this range. The fabric is wetted and dried during the dyeing process, which encourages slight tightening of the weave. As a result, most batiks have a smooth texture or hand, which in combination with the dense thread count ensures clarity of design.

Another result of the extensive batik production process is that the fabric has slightly less give than other quilting cottons when easing pieces together. This is actually a benefit, as batik pieces cut on the bias hardly stretch at all. Your pieces will fit together with no problem if you cut them accurately and take care to use an accurate seam allowance.

DYES

TRADITIONALLY, dyes for printing batiks were made from plants, limiting the color choices. Now, with the use of modern inks and chemical dyes, you can find everything from vibrant reds and black to bold chartreuse. These dyes have not only improved the color range of batiks but they have also improved the color stability. Synthetic dyes bleed less, are more colorfast, and retain their brilliance after washing.

Concerns over colorfastness shouldn't be any more intense with batiks than with other fabric. For the batik manufacturer, getting the wax off the cloth involves rinsing it in boiling hot water, which also washes out most of the excess dye. Still, even the most reputable companies will occasionally produce a batik that bleeds in the wash. Prewashing is recommended (see "Preparing Your Fabrics" on page 15).

Many fabrics classified as batiks are actually hand-dyed fabrics. Hand-dyed fabrics and solid-looking, one-color textured batiks generally don't require the use of wax to create their texture, so they may not have been boiled and may not be as colorfast as a true batik. Again, prewashing is recommended.

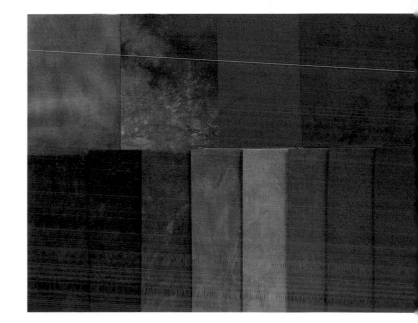

Hand-Dyed Fabrics

CHOOSING FABRICS

FABRIC SELECTION is the key to a successful quilt. You'll notice that many of the quilts in this book are centered around one main multicolored batik—often the border fabric. A multicolored fabric with a medium to large print can serve as the inspiration for the entire color scheme of a quilt. I recommend that you pick this fabric first for your project and then select other fabrics to coordinate with it. Many companies are making batiks, and the variety of styles available is enormous. Below are examples of batiks as well as traditional quilting cottons that would provide excellent inspiration. Look also for inspiration in items from your everyday life. You may find color and design ideas in something as simple as your bathroom tiles or a page from a magazine.

Batik Main Fabrics

Nonbatik Main Fabrics

This photo was taken during my trip to the Southwest and was the inspiration for "Sedona Sunrise" (page 44). The colors are not exactly the same, but the mood is there.

The fabric in this little bag inspired the design for "Mixed Up but Not Crazy" (page 54). I couldn't quite make the colors in the bag work, but it did give me the idea for the quilt.

You can also take inspiration right from the fabric manufacturer. Often fabrics will come in coordinated color groups, making the selection almost preordained, if you care to go that route. Working with coordinated groupings is a good option if you feel inexperienced or you just aren't comfortable selecting fabrics on your own.

Some quilts in this book, like "Spice Market" (page 16) and "So, What Color Is Teal, Exactly?" (page 58) are centered around a color sequence. In these cases, there isn't one dominating multicolored fabric; there's just a series of fabrics that make a good progression or overall blend.

Detail of "Spice Market"

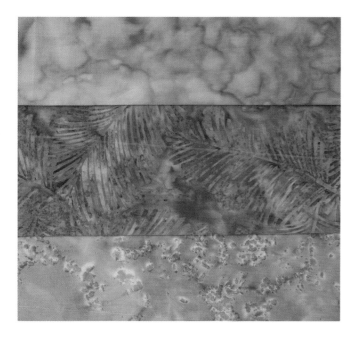

The fabric in the center was used for the border of "Whirlwind" (page 81). The mottled fabrics on each side of the border fabric are part of the same color group.

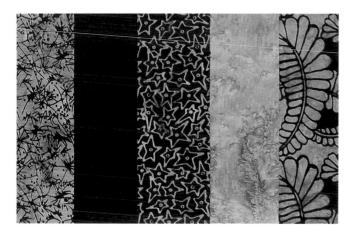

This coordinated fabric group includes large- and medium-size prints and solids and would make a wonderfully striking quilt such as "Pineapple Princess" (page 23) or "Noshi for Long Life" (page 74).

Fabrics Used in "So, What Color Is Teal, Exactly?"

Main fabrics don't always have to be multicolored. In "Red Sky at Night" (page 46), I knew I wanted to use an incredible two-color print but was afraid it wouldn't have any appeal. With a relatively simple pattern and two coordinating solid batiks, a very effective quilt emerged.

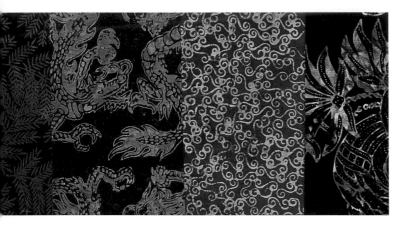

Inspiring Two-Color Fabrics

Once you have your main print fabric or color scheme, take direction from the colors in the main fabric to choose the rest of your fabrics, making sure to include a variety of textures. Keep in mind that if all of the prints are similar in scale, the quilt may appear either too flat or too busy. Vary the size of the prints and include fabrics that read solid for a place where the eyes can rest.

When you're selecting fabrics, keep in mind that there are no right or wrong choices. You don't have to adhere to a color wheel or pick lights, mediums, and darks for each quilt. Try combining different genres of fabrics: batiks, Asian prints, large florals, and small conservative prints. Choose fabrics that you like, that make you feel good, or that achieve the desired effect. Don't be intimidated by the worry that you aren't choosing the correct fabrics. Remember, quilting is a learning process. If you can't just "go with it," try making up one or two blocks, or a small section of the quilt, using the fabrics you select. Step back and see what you think!

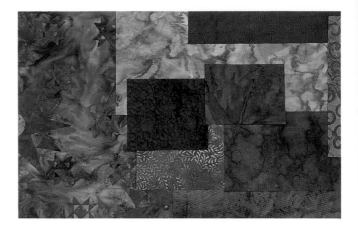

The fabric selection used in "Patchwork Puzzle" (page 88) includes a large-print multicolor border, a few small prints, and solid textures. The values range from medium light to dark.

Create a stunning palette with a mixture of fabric types. This selection features a range of groups, including Asian prints, batiks, small-scale traditional quilting cottons, and tone-on-tone hand-dyed fabrics.

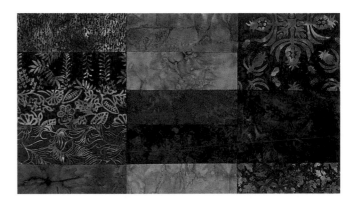

You can choose a palette of mostly the same value as I did in "Arboretum in Autumn" (page 66). They may be all on the dark side, but what a rich, luxurious quilt they can make with lots of interesting detail.

PREPARING YOUR FABRICS

ALL FABRICS, including batiks, should be prewashed in order to preshrink them, remove any sizing that may have been added during the manufacturing process, and test for colorfastness. You can prewash fabrics by hand or machine. Keep similar values and colors together and wash the fabrics on a short gentle cycle, using a small amount of commercial detergent or, preferably, a gentle soap made especially for quilting fabrics. Use cool water and check the water during the final rinse to see if it is running clear (no color). If it isn't, put the fabric through another rinse cycle. Continue until the water runs clear. If you come across a fabric that continues to bleed, add a cup of white vinegar to the rinse water to help set the dye. There are also chemical products available at your quilt shop that aid in removing excess dye and setting the color in the fabric.

To dry fabrics, I recommend using the hot setting on the dryer. Run the cycle until the fabric is just dry, to encourage the most shrinkage. To prevent wrinkles from setting, remove the fabric promptly before it has a chance to sit in the dryer. Using a hot iron, press the entire length of fabric, always pressing parallel to the selvage.

For each quilt project in this book, the yardage amounts listed under "Materials" allow for shrinkage and straightening and assume a 40" fabric width after prewashing. If your fabric measures less than 40" wide after preshrinking, you may need additional fabric. Note that directional designs may also require additional fabric and/or a change in the cutting direction.

SPICE MARKET

By Laurie Shifrin, twin size, 57½" x 75½". Machine quilted by Becky Kraus. Lush cinnamons and creamy golds, as well as the sparkly border print, make you feel as if you're looking at the varied bowls of ground spices at a market in India. Twinkling triangles draw your eye from fabric to fabric.

QUILT FACTS

	Crib/Lap	Twin	Queen/King
Finished quilt size	43¼" x 56¾"	57½" x 75½"	81¼" x 106¾"

MATERIALS

Yardage is based on 40"-wide fabric. Fabrics are numbered from the center of the quilt out.

	Crib/Lap	Twin	Queen/King
Fabric 1: Rust print batik for quilt top	⅜ yard	⅜ yard	½ yard
Fabric 2: Beige batik for quilt top	¼ yard	¼ yard	¼ yard
Fabric 3: Gold flower-print batik for quilt top	¼ yard	¼ yard	¼ yard
Fabric 4: Gold batik for quilt top	⅝ yard	⅞ yard	1⅜ yards
Fabric 5: Rust leaf-print batik for quilt top	⅜ yard	½ yard	½ yard
Fabric 6: Gold print batik for quilt top center	⅜ yard	½ yard	½ yard
Fabric 7: Dark cinnamon batik for quilt top	¾ yard	1⅛ yards	2 yards
Fabric 8: Orange print batik for quilt top	½ yard	½ yard	⅝ yard
Fabric 9: Brown print batik for quilt top	½ yard	½ yard	⅝ yard
Fabric 10: Tan ornate-print batik for quilt top	⅝ yard	⅞ yard	1⅜ yards
Fabric 11: Brick red batik for quilt top	¼ yard	½ yard	⅝ yard
Fabric 12: Tan print batik for quilt top and border	⅜ yard	½ yard	¾ yard
Fabric 13: Brown swirly-print batik for border	1⅛ yards	1¾ yards	3⅛ yards
Backing	3 yards	4⅞ yards	7⅞ yards
Binding	⅝ yard	¾ yard	⅞ yard
Batting	50" x 63"	64" x 82"	88" x 113"

CUTTING

All measurements include ¼"-wide seam allowances.

	Piece Dimensions		
	Crib/Lap	Twin	Queen/King
Fabric 1			
1. Cut 1 strip:	7¼" x 40"	9½" x 40"	13¼" x 40"
2. Crosscut into 1 square (A):	7¼" x 7¼"	9½" x 9½"	13¼" x 13¼"
3. From the remainder of the strip, cut 4 squares (B):	2¾" x 2¾"	3½" x 3½"	4¾" x 4¾"
Fabrics 2 and 3			
1. Cut 1 strip from *each* of fabrics 2 and 3:	3½" x 40"	4¼" x 40"	5½" x 40"
2. Crosscut *each* strip into 2 squares (C):	3½" x 3½"	4¼" x 4¼"	5½" x 5½"
3. Trim remainder of *each* strip to:	3⅛" wide (D)	3⅞" wide (D)	5⅛" wide (D)

CUTTING (continued)

All measurements include ¼"-wide seam allowances.

	Piece Dimensions		
	Crib/Lap	**Twin**	**Queen/King**
Fabric 4			
1. For crib/lap or twin, cut 2 strips:	5" x 40"	6½" x 40"	—
For queen/king, cut 3 strips:	—	—	9" x 40"
2. Crosscut strips into 4 rectangles (E):	5" x 7¼"	6½" x 9½"	9" x 13¼"
4 squares (F):	5" x 5"	6½" x 6½"	9" x 9"
3. For crib/lap or twin, cut 2 strips:	2¾" x 40"	3½" x 40"	—
For queen/king, cut 3 strips:	—	—	4¾" x 40"
4. Crosscut strips into 20 squares (B):	2¾" x 2¾"	3½" x 3½"	4¾" x 4¾"
Fabrics 5 and 6			
1. Cut 1 strip from *each* of fabrics 5 and 6:	3½" x 40"	4¼" x 40"	5½" x 40"
2. Crosscut *each* strip into 2 squares (C):	3½" x 3½"	4¼" x 4¼"	5½" x 5½"
3. Trim remainder of each strip to:	3⅛" wide (D)	3⅞" wide (D)	5⅛" wide (D)
4. Cut 1 strip (D) from *each* of fabrics 5 and 6:	3⅛" x 40"	3⅞" x 40"	5⅛" x 40"
Fabric 7			
1. For crib/lap, cut 2 strips:	5" x 40"	—	—
For twin, cut 3 strips:	—	6½" x 40"	—
For queen/king, cut 4 strips:	—	—	9" x 40"
2. Crosscut strips into 2 rectangles (E):	5" x 7¼"	6½" x 9½"	9" x 13¼"
12 squares (F):	5" x 5"	6½" x 6½"	9" x 9"
3. For crib/lap and twin, cut 3 strips:	2¾" x 40"	3½" x 40"	—
For queen/king, cut 4 strips:	—	—	4¾" x 40"
4. Crosscut strips into 30 squares (B):	2¾" x 2¾"	3½" x 3½"	4¾" x 4¾"
Fabrics 8 and 9			
1. Cut 1 strip from *each* of fabrics 8 and 9:	3½" x 40"	4¼" x 40"	5½" x 40"
2. Crosscut *each* strip into 1 square (C):	3½" x 3½"	4¼" x 4¼"	5½" x 5½"
3. Trim remainder of *each* strip to:	3⅛" wide (D)	3⅞" wide (D)	5⅛" wide (D)
4. For crib/lap and twin, cut 1 strip (D) from *each* of fabrics 8 and 9:	3⅛" x 40"	3⅞" x 40"	—
For queen/king, cut 2 strips (D) from *each* of fabrics 8 and 9:	—	—	5⅛" x 40"
Fabric 10			
1. Cut 2 strips:	5" x 40"	6½" x 40"	9" x 40"
2. Crosscut strips into 8 squares (F):	5" x 5"	6½" x 6½"	9" x 9"
3. For crib/lap, cut 2 strips:	2¾" x 40"	—	—
For twin, cut 3 strips:	—	3½" x 40"	—
For queen/king, cut 4 strips:	—	—	4¾" x 40"
4. Crosscut strips into 4 rectangles (G):	2¾" x 7¼"	3½" x 9½"	4¾" x 13¼"
16 squares (B):	2¾" x 2¾"	3½" x 3½"	4¾" x 4¾"

CUTTING (continued)

All measurements include ¼"-wide seam allowances.

	Piece Dimensions		
	Crib/Lap	Twin	Queen/King
Fabric 11			
For crib/lap, cut 1 strip (D):	3⅛" x 40"	—	—
For twin and queen/king, cut 2 strips (D):	—	3⅞" x 40"	5⅛" x 40"
Fabric 12			
For crib/lap and twin, cut 2 strips (D):	3⅛" x 40"	3⅞" x 40"	—
For queen/king, cut 3 strips (D):	—	—	5⅛" x 40"
Fabric 13			
1. For crib/lap, cut 4 strips:	5" x 40"	—	—
For twin, cut 6 strips:	—	6½" x 40"	—
For queen/king, cut 8 strips:	—	—	9" x 40"
2. Crosscut strips into 2 rectangles (H):	5" x 25¼"	6½" x 33½"	9" x 47¼"
			(cut from 3 pieced strips)
4 rectangles (I):	5" x 11¾"	6½" x 15½"	9" x 21¾"
4 rectangles (E):	5" x 7¼"	6½" x 9½"	9" x 13¼"
4 squares (F):	5" x 5"	6½" x 6½"	9" x 9"
3. For crib/lap and twin, cut 1 strip (D):	3⅛" x 40"	3⅞" x 40"	—
For queen/king, cut 2 strips (D):	—	—	5⅛" x 40"
4. For crib/lap and twin, cut 2 strips:	2¾" x 40"	3½" x 40"	—
For queen/king, cut 3 strips:	—	—	4¾" x 40"
5. Crosscut strips into 18 squares (B):	2¾" x 2¾"	3½" x 3½"	4¾" x 4¾"
Binding fabric			
For crib/lap, cut 6 strips:	2½" x 40"	—	—
For twin, cut 7 strips:	—	2½" x 40"	—
For queen/king, cut 10 strips:	—	—	2½" x 40"

QUILT-TOP ASSEMBLY

1. Using the D strips, refer to "Multiple Half-Square-Triangle Units" on page 99 to make 8 units from fabrics 2 and 3, 24 units from fabrics 5 and 6, 28 units from fabrics 8 and 9, 24 units from fabrics 11 and 12, and 16 units from fabrics 12 and 13.

Make 8. Make 24. Make 28. Make 24. Make 16.

2. Using the C squares, refer to "Quarter-Square-Triangle Units" on page 99 to make four units from fabrics 2 and 3, four units from fabrics 5 and 6, and two units from fabrics 8 and 9.

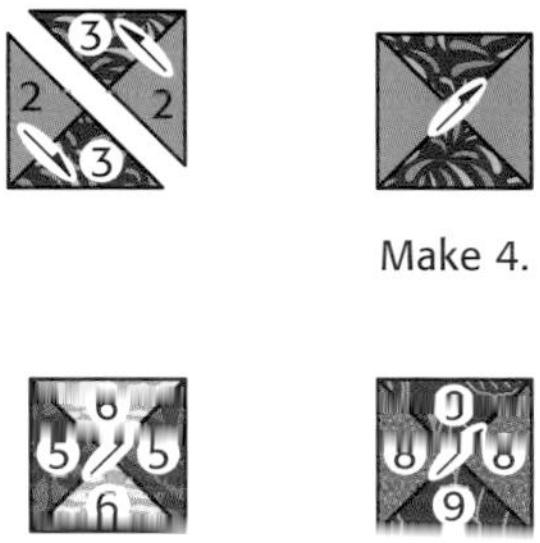

Make 4.

Make 4. Make 2.

3. Using the B squares from fabric 1, eight of the B squares from fabric 4, and the fabric 2-3 half-square- and quarter-square-triangle units from steps 1 and 2, make four units as shown.

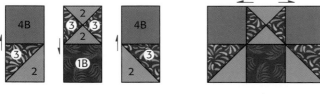

Make 4.

4. Repeat step 3 to make four units as shown, using the B squares from fabric 1, the B squares from fabric 7, and the fabric 5-6 half-square- and quarter-square-triangle units.

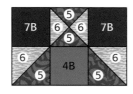

Make 4.

5. Make eight units as shown, using the B squares from fabric 4, the B squares from fabric 7, and the fabric 5-6 half-square-triangle units.

Make 8.

6. Repeat step 5 to make 12 units as shown, using the B squares from fabric 7, the B squares from fabric 10, and the fabric 8-9 half-square-triangle units.

Make 12.

7. Using the B squares from fabric 10 and the fabric 11-12 half-square-triangle units, make four units as shown.

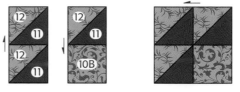

Make 4.

8. Arrange the units for the quilt-top center as shown to make 11 horizontal rows. Stitch the units in each row together. Sew the rows together.

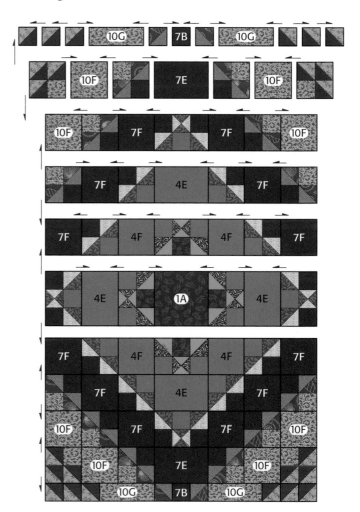

BORDER ASSEMBLY AND FINISHING

1. Using the fabric 12-13 half-square-triangle units from step 1 of "Quilt-Top Assembly" and the B squares from fabric 13, make eight units as shown.

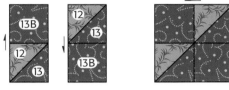

Make 8.

2. Make the border units as shown, using the units from step 1; the B, E, F, H, and I pieces from fabric 13; and the fabric 8-9 quarter-square-triangle units. Make two side border units and two top and bottom border units.

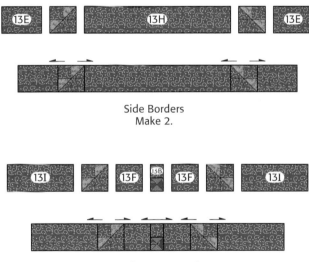

Side Borders
Make 2.

Top and Bottom Borders
Make 2.

3. Refer to "Adding Borders" on page 101 to attach the borders to the quilt-top sides and then the top and bottom edges, matching seams.

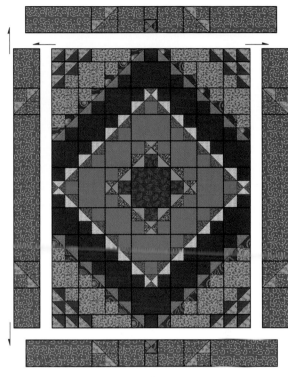

Quilt Assembly Diagram

4. Refer to "Finishing" on pages 102–109 to layer the quilt top with batting and backing; baste. Quilt as desired. Bind the edges and add a label.

ALTERNATE QUILT

CRIB/LAP SIZE

PURPLE MOSAIC, by Laurie Shifrin, 43¼" x 56¾".
Machine quilted by Kathy Staley.
What a great way to spotlight a Japanese pictorial fabric: using it as the focal point in this quilt's center medallion. Asian prints blended with small florals and batiks dazzle the eye.

PINEAPPLE PRINCESS

By Laurie Shifrin, lap/twin size, 61" x 72". Machine quilted by Becky Kraus. When I was about six or seven years old, I used to put on a grass hula skirt and sing "Pineapple Princess" to anyone who would listen. I have no memory of doing this, but my aunts swear to it. This quilt, in all of its boldness and lush greenness, reminds me of the splendors of Hawaii and what I must have been feeling when I performed that song.

QUILT FACTS

	Crib	Lap/Twin	Double/Queen	King
Finished quilt size	50" x 50"	61" x 72"	83" x 94"	105" x 116"
Finished block size	5½" x 5½"	5½" x 5½"	5½" x 5½"	5½" x 5½"
Number of pieced blocks	33	58	110	178

MATERIALS

Yardage is based on 40"-wide fabric.

	Crib	Lap/Twin	Double/Queen	King
At least 10 bright batik prints for pieced blocks	¼ yard *each*	⅜ yard *each*	½ yard *each*	⅝ yard *each*
Green solid batik for background	1⅝ yards	3 yards	5¼ yards	8½ yards
Floral-print batik for inner border	1 yard	1⅜ yards	1⅝ yards	2 yards
Backing	3⅜ yards	4 yards	7¾ yards	10½ yards
Binding	⅝ yard	¾ yard	⅞ yard	1 yard
Batting	56" x 56"	67" x 78"	89" x 100"	111" x 122"

CUTTING

All measurements include ¼"-wide seam allowances.

	Number to Cut			
	Crib	Lap/Twin	Double/Queen	King
Bright batik prints				
1. Cut 4¼" x 4¼" squares (C):	33 *total*	58 *total*	110 *total*	178 *total*
2. Cut 1¾" x 1¾" squares (A):	132 *total*	232 *total*	440 *total*	712 *total*
Green solid batik				
1. Cut 6" x 40" strips:	4	9	17	29
2. Crosscut 6" x 40" strips into 6" x 6" squares (D):	24	49	101	169
3. Cut 3½" x 40" strips:	6	11	20	33
4. Crosscut 3½" x 40" strips into 1¾" x 3½" rectangles (B):	132	232	440	712

CUTTING (continued)

All measurements include ¼"-wide seam allowances.

	Number to Cut			
	Crib	**Lap/Twin**	**Double/Queen**	**King**
Floral-print batik				
1. For crib and lap/twin, cut 6" x 40" strips:	4	6	—	—
For double/queen and king, cut 6" x length of fabric strips:	—	—	5	5
2. Crosscut strips into				
6" x 6" squares (D):	4	4	4	4
6" x 11½" rectangles (E):	4	4	4	4
6" x 17" strips (F):	4	—	—	—
6" x 28" strips (F):	—	2	—	—
6" x 39" strips (G and F):	—	2 (G)	2 (F)	—
6" x 50" strips (G and F):	—	—	2 (G)	2 (F)
6" x 61" strips (G):	—	—	—	2
Binding fabric				
Cut 2½" x 40" strips:	6	8	10	12

QUILT-TOP ASSEMBLY AND FINISHING

1. To make the center squares of the pieced blocks, refer to "Quarter-Square-Triangle Units" on page 99 to make quarter-square-triangle units using the 4¼" C squares. Pair each square with a square of a different color. Once you sew the squares and cut them into triangle pairs, rearrange the triangle pairs to make units. Refer to "Quilt Facts" on page 24 to make the same number of units as the number of pieced blocks for the quilt size you are making.

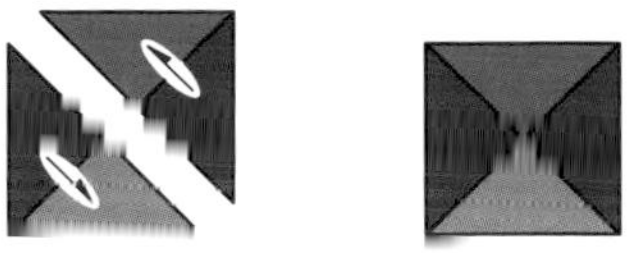

2. Sew a B rectangle to opposite sides of each of the units from step 1.

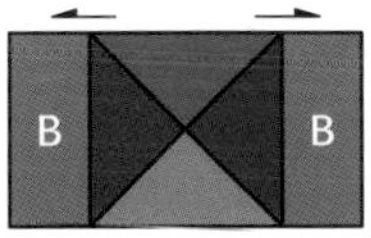

3. Stitch matching A squares to the ends of two B rectangles. Repeat with the remaining B rectangles.

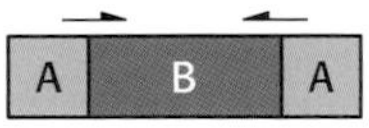

4. Attach matching pieced strips from step 3 to the top and bottom edges of the units from step 2 to complete the blocks.

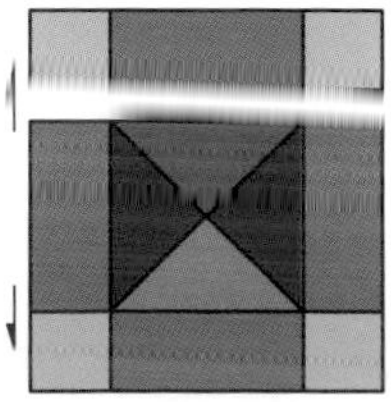

5. Refer to the illustrations below and the quilt assembly diagram for the size quilt you are making to arrange the pieced blocks, D squares, and E, F, and G border pieces as shown. Stitch the pieces together into rows. Sew the rows together. Press all seams away from the pieced blocks.

NOTE: *The pressing instructions and quilt assembly diagram shown in the illustrations below are for the lap/twin quilt. Assemby diagrams for other quilt sizes are shown on page 27.*

6. Refer to "Finishing" on pages 102–109 to layer the quilt top with batting and backing; baste. Quilt as desired. Bind the edges and add a label.

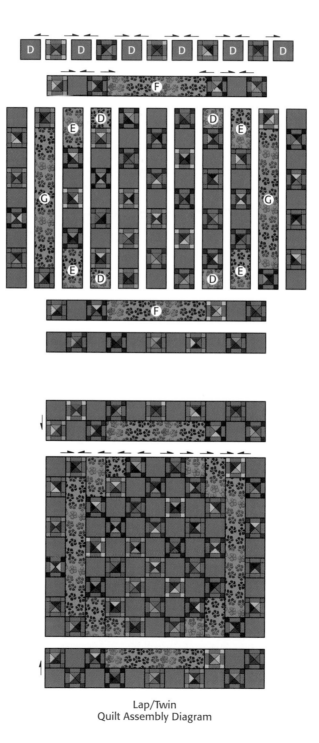

Lap/Twin
Quilt Assembly Diagram

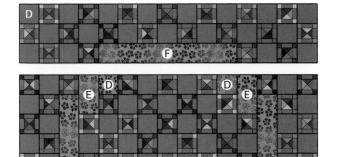

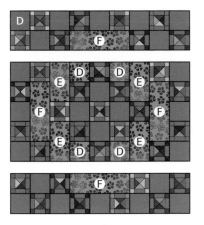

Crib
Quilt Assembly Diagram

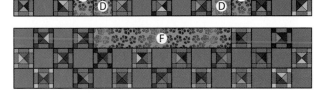

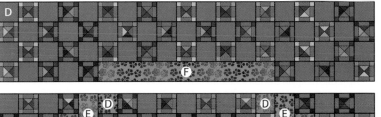

Double/Queen
Quilt Assembly Diagram

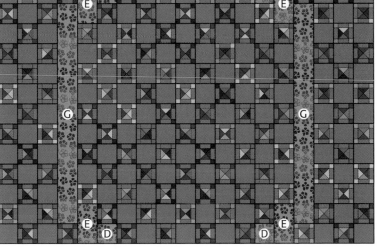

King
Quilt Assembly Diagram

ALTERNATE QUILT

DOUBLE/QUEEN SIZE

RUBY MEDALLION, by Laurie Shifrin, 83" x 94".
Machine quilted by Sherry Rogers.
Rich reds and numerous golds form an elegant quilt that would look lovely centered over
any bed. The traditional designs of this quilt are combined and transformed into one that is a
true classic.

TERRA-COTTA DREAMS

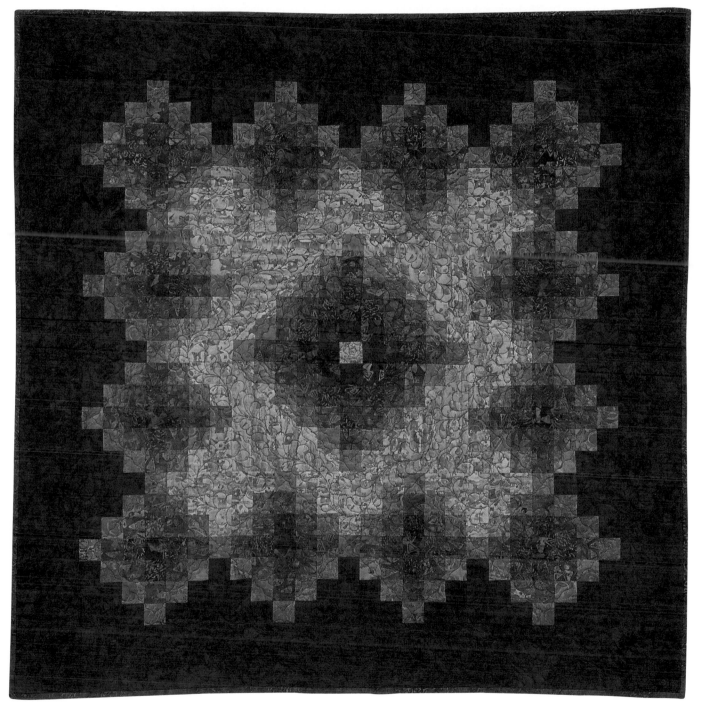

By Laurie Shifrin, crib/wall-hanging size, 47" x 47". Machine quilted by Sherry Rogers. The Trip around the World pattern has always been a favorite of mine, and I am always looking for ways to create new patterns using the old standard. The earthen colors of this quilt softly blend together, while the center trip appears to be suspended and floating above the light claylike background.

QUILT FACTS

	Crib/Wall Hanging	Twin/Double
Finished quilt size	47" x 47"	62½" x 86½"

MATERIALS

Yardage is based on 40"-wide fabric.

	Crib/Wall Hanging	Twin/Double
Fabric 1: Dark batik	¼ yard	¼ yard
Fabric 2: Medium-dark batik	⅜ yard	⅝ yard
Fabric 3: Medium batik	⅝ yard	1 yard
Fabric 4: Medium-light batik	¾ yard	1¼ yards
Fabric 5: Very dark batik	1¾ yards	2⅞ yards
Fabric 6: Light batik	¾ yard	1¾ yards
Backing	3¼ yards	5½ yards
Binding	⅝ yard	¾ yard
Batting	53" x 53"	69" x 93"

CUTTING

All measurements include ¼"-wide seam allowances.

	Piece Dimensions	
	Crib/Wall Hanging	Twin/Double
Fabric 1		
1. Cut 2 strips:	2" x 40"	2½" x 40"
2. Cut 1 strip in half crosswise to yield 2 strips:	2" x 20" (1 left over)	2½" x 20"
Fabric 2		
1. For crib/wall hanging, cut 4 strips:	2" x 40"	—
For twin/double, cut 6 strips:	—	2½" x 40"
2. For crib/wall hanging, cut 1 strip in half crosswise to yield 2 strips:	2" x 20"	—
For twin/double, cut 2 strips in half crosswise to yield 4 strips:	—	2½" x 20"
Fabric 3		
1. For crib/wall hanging, cut 7 strips:	2" x 40"	—
For twin/double, cut 11 strips:	—	2½" x 40"
2. For crib/wall hanging, cut 2 strips in half crosswise to yield 4 strips:	2" x 20"	—
For twin/double, cut 3 strips in half crosswise to yield 6 strips:	—	2½" x 20"
Fabric 4		
1. For crib/wall hanging, cut 10 strips:	2" x 40"	—
For twin/double, cut 15 strips:	—	2½" x 40"
2. Cut 4 strips in half crosswise to yield 8 strips:	2" x 20" (1 left over)	2½" x 20"

CUTTING (continued)

All measurements include ¼"-wide seam allowances.

	Piece Dimensions	
	Crib/Wall Hanging	**Twin/Double**
Fabric 5		
1. For crib/wall hanging, cut 7 strips:	5" x 40"	—
For twin/double, cut 10 strips:	—	6½" x 40"
2. For crib/wall hanging, cut 2 strips in half crosswise to yield 4 strips:	5" x 20" (1 left over)	—
For twin/double, cut 1 strip in half crosswise to yield 2 strips:	—	6½" x 20"
3. For crib/wall hanging, cut 2 strips:	3½" x 40"	—
For twin/double, cut 3 strips:	—	4½" x 40"
4. Cut 1 strip in half crosswise to yield 2 strips:	3½" x 20"	4½" x 20"
5. Cut 3 strips:	2" x 40"	2½" x 40"
6. Crosscut 1 strip into 2 strips:	2" x 20"	2½" x 20"
Crosscut 1 strip into 4 squares:	2" x 2"	2½" x 2½"
Fabric 6		
1. For crib/wall hanging, cut 1 strip:	8⅜" x 40"	—
For twin/double, cut 2 strips:	—	12½" x 40"
2. For crib/wall hanging, crosscut strip into		
2 squares:	8⅜" x 8⅜"	—
• Trim remainder of strip to:	5" wide	
• Cut 1 strip:	5" x 20"	—
For twin/double, cut strips into		
2 rectangles:	—	12½" x 22½"
2 squares:	—	10⅞" x 10⅞"
3. Cut each square from step 2 in half once diagonally to yield 4 half-square triangles.		
4. For twin/double, cut 1 strip:	—	6½" x 40"
5. For crib/wall hanging, cut 1 strip:	3½" x 40"	—
For twin/double, cut 2 strips:	—	4½" x 40"
6. Cut 1 strip:	2⅜" x 40"	2⅞" x 40"
7. Crosscut strip from step 6 into 10 squares:	2⅜" x 2⅜"	2⅞" x 2⅞"
8. Cut each square from step 7 in half once diagonally to yield 20 half-square triangles.		
9. From the remainder of the strip from step 6,		
cut 1 square:	2" x 2"	2½" x 2½"
10. For crib/wall hanging, cut 1 strip:	2" x 40"	—
For twin/double, cut 2 strips:	—	2½" x 40"
Binding fabric		
For crib/wall hanging, cut 6 strips:	2½" x 40"	—
For twin/double, cut 8 strips:	—	2½" x 40

QUILT-TOP ASSEMBLY FOR CRIB/WALL-HANGING SIZE

1. Sew 2" x 20" strips of fabrics 1, 2, 3, and 4 together as shown to make one strip set. From the strip set, cut six segments, 2" wide, for the center trip.

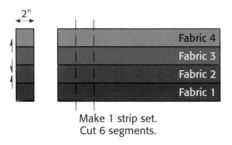

Make 1 strip set.
Cut 6 segments.

2. Stitch 2" x 40" strips of fabrics 1, 2, 3, and 4 together as shown to make one strip set. From the strip set, cut 14 segments, 2" wide. You will use 12 segments for the outer trips and 2 for the center trip.

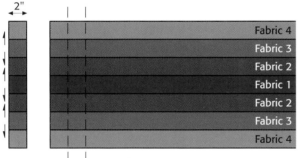

Make 1 strip set.
Cut 14 segments.

3. Using 2" x 40" strips and 3½" x 40" strips, make one each of the following strip sets. From *each* strip-set combination, cut 20 segments, 2" wide, for the outer trips.

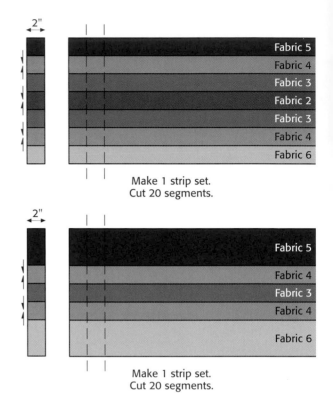

Make 1 strip set.
Cut 20 segments.

Make 1 strip set.
Cut 20 segments.

4. Using 2" x 20" strips of fabrics 2, 3, and 4, make one strip set as shown. From the strip set, cut 2 segments, 2" wide, for the center trip.

Make 1 strip set.
Cut 2 segments.

Stitch 2" x 20" strips of fabric 5 to the top and bottom edges of the remainder of the strip set as shown. From the new strip set, cut four segments, 2" wide, for the outer trips.

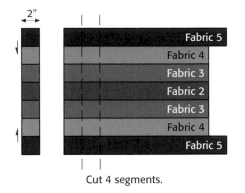

Cut 4 segments.

5. Sew 2" x 20" strips of fabrics 3 and 4 together to make one strip set as shown. From the strip set, cut two segments, 2" wide, for the center trip. Stitch 3½" x 20" strips of fabric 5 to the top and bottom edges of the remainder of the strip set as shown. From the new strip set, cut four segments, 2" wide, for the outer trips.

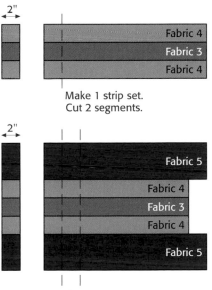

Make 1 strip set.
Cut 2 segments.

Cut 4 segments.

6. From a 2" x 20" strip of fabric 4, cut two squares, 2" x 2", for the center trip. Stitch a 5" x 20" strip of fabric 5 to both long edges of the remainder of the strip to make a strip set. From the strip set, cut four segments, 2" wide.

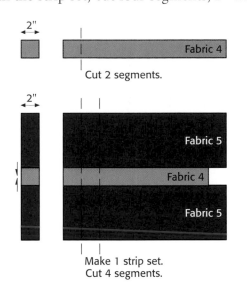

Cut 2 segments.

Make 1 strip set.
Cut 4 segments.

7. Sew one 2" x 20" strip of fabric 4 and one 5" x 20" strip *each* of fabrics 5 and 6 together to make one strip set as shown. From the strip set, cut 8 segments, 2" wide, for the outer trips.

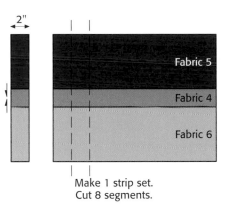

Make 1 strip set.
Cut 8 segments.

8. To finish assembling the rows for the center trip, sew two 1-2-3-4 segments from step 1, two 2" squares of fabric 5, and one 2" square of fabric 6 together as shown. Make one. Make two rows using two 1-2-3-4 segments and one 2" square of fabric 5.

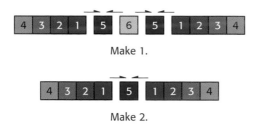

Make 1.

Make 2.

9. Lay out the rows for the center trip as shown. Sew a 2⅜" half-square triangle of fabric 6 to the ends of each row, being careful to orient the triangles correctly. Sew the rows together.

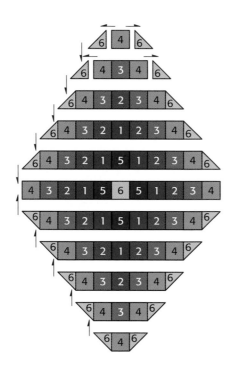

10. Attach the 8⅜" half-square triangles of fabric 6 to the sides of the center trip.

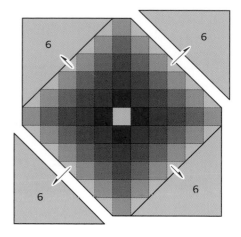

11. To make the outer-trip side panels, sew the strip-set segments together as shown. Make two.

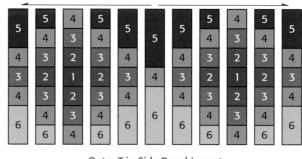

Outer-Trip Side Panel Layout
Make 2.

12. To make the outer-trip top and bottom panels, sew the remaining strip-set segments together as shown below. Make two.

13. Refer to the quilt assembly diagram on page 36 to stitch the quilt-top units together, matching seams.

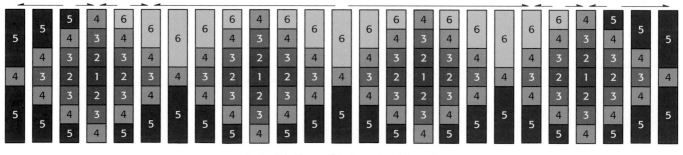

Outer-Trip Top and Bottom Panel Layout
Make 2.

QUILT-TOP ASSEMBLY FOR TWIN/DOUBLE SIZE

1. Refer to step 1 of the crib/wall-hanging instructions to make one strip set using 2½" x 20" strips. From the strip set, cut six segments, 2½" wide, for the center trip.

2. Refer to step 2 of the crib/wall-hanging instructions to make one strip set using the 2½" x 40" strips. Make one additional strip set using the 2½" x 20" strips. From the strip sets, cut 18 segments, 2½" wide. You will use 16 segments for the outer trips and 2 for the center trip.

3. Refer to step 3 of the crib/wall-hanging instructions to make two of each strip set using the 2½" x 40" strips and 4½" x 40" strips. From each strip-set combination, cut 28 segments, 2½" wide, for the outer trips.

4. Repeat step 4 of the crib/wall-hanging instructions, using 2½" x 20" strips and cutting 2½"-wide segments.

5. Refer to step 5 of the crib/wall-hanging instructions to make one strip set using the 2½" x 20" strips. From the strip set, cut two segments, 2½" wide, for the center trip. Stitch a 4½" x 20" strip of fabric 5 to the top and bottom edges of the remainder of the strip set as shown. From the new strip set, cut four segments, 2½" wide, for the outer trips.

6. Refer to step 6 of the crib/wall-hanging instructions to cut two squares, 2½" x 2½" from a 2½" x 20" strip of fabric 4. Stitch a 6½" x 20" strip of fabric 5 to the top and bottom edges of the remainder of the strip. From the strip set, cut four segments, 2½" wide.

7. Refer to step 7 of the crib/wall-hanging instructions to sew 2½" x 40" and 6½" x 40" strips together to make one strip set. From the strip set, cut 12 segments, 2½" wide, for the outer trips.

8. Repeat step 8 of the crib/wall-hanging instructions, using 2½" squares.

9. Repeat step 9 of the crib/wall-hanging instructions, using 2⅞" half-square triangles at the ends of each row.

10. Repeat step 10 of the crib/wall-hanging instructions, using the 10⅞" half-square triangles. Sew a 12½" x 22½" rectangle of fabric 6 to the top and bottom edges of the center trip unit.

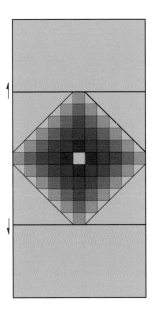

11. To make the outer-trip side panels, sew the strip-set segments together as shown below. Make two.

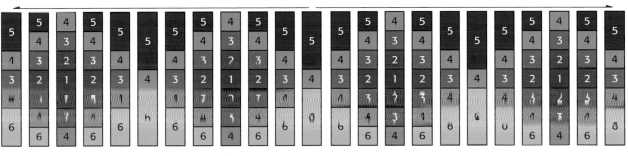

Twin/Double Outer-Trip Side Panel Layout
Make 2.

12. Repeat step 12 of the crib/wall-hanging instructions to make two outer-trip top and bottom panels.

13. Refer to the quilt assembly diagram to stitch the quilt-top units together, matching seams.

ATTACHING THE BORDERS AND FINISHING

1. Using the 5"-wide strips of fabric 5 for the crib/wall-hanging size or the 6½"-wide strips of fabric 5 for the twin/double size, refer to "Adding Borders" on page 101 to measure and trim the border strips and sew them to the quilt top, piecing the strips as necessary to achieve the required length.

2. Refer to "Finishing" on pages 102–109 to layer the quilt top with batting and backing; baste. Quilt as desired. Bind the edges; add a label.

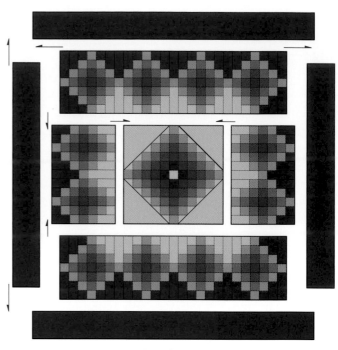

Crib/Wall Hanging
Quilt Assembly Diagram

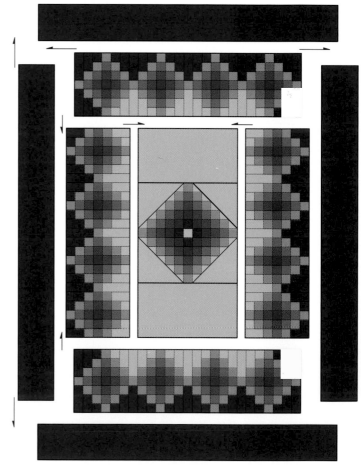

Twin/Double
Quilt Assembly Diagram

ALTERNATE QUILT

TWIN/DOUBLE SIZE

MOROCCAN CARPET, by Laurie Shifrin, 62½" x 86½".
Machine quilted by Sherry Rogers. Lush reds contrast with dazzling oranges in this bold combination of batiks and traditional cottons. Large unpieced spaces provide an opportunity to show off your favorite fabrics, or if you dare, to serve as a background for your favorite appliqué patterns.

REACH FOR THE STARS

By Laurie Shifrin, lap/twin size, 60½" x 60½". Machine quilted by Sherry Rogers. A pale yellow batik background sets off the Flying Geese blocks that are combined with bold eight-pointed stars to create this dynamic quilt. You can decide if the shapes formed by the two shades of green more closely resemble a Pineapple Log Cabin block or trees in a forest.

QUILT FACTS

	Crib/Wall Hanging	Lap/Twin
Finished quilt size	35½" x 35½"	60½" x 60½"
Finished Chain Square block size	7½" x 7½"	7½" x 7½"
Finished Flying Geese block size	5" x 7½"	5" x 7½"
Finished Square-in-a-Square block size	5" x 5"	5" x 5"

MATERIALS

Yardage is based on 40"-wide fabric.

	Crib/Wall Hanging	Lap/Twin
Fabric 1: Medium green print batik for blocks and inner border	½ yard	⅞ yard
Fabric 2: Dark green batik for blocks	⅜ yard	1⅛ yards
Fabric 3: Medium peach batik for blocks	¼ yard	⅜ yard
Fabric 4: Plum batik for stars	½ yard	⅞ yard
Fabric 5: Yellow batik for background	¼ yard	1½ yards
Fabric 6: Multicolor print batik for inner border, outer border, and Square-in-a-Square blocks	1¼ yards	1⅝ yards
Fabric 7: Light peach print batik for center Square-in-a-Square block	—	5" x 5" scrap
Backing	2⅜ yards	4 yards
Binding	½ yard	¾ yard
Batting	42" x 42"	67" x 67"

CUTTING

All measurements include ¼"-wide seam allowances.

	Number to Cut	
	Crib/Wall Hanging	Lap/Twin
Fabric 1		
1. Cut 6¼" x 40" strip(s):	1	2
2. Crosscut into 6¼" x 6¼" squares:	3	12
3. Cut each square in half twice diagonally to yield quarter-square triangles (B):	12	48
4. Cut 2" x 40" strips:	2	4
5. For crib/wall hanging, crosscut into 2" x 18" rectangles (H):	8	—
For lap/twin, crosscut into 2" x 18" rectangles (H):	—	8

CUTTING (continued)

All measurements include ¼"-wide seam allowances.

	Number to Cut	
	Crib	**Lap/Twin**
Fabric 2		
1. Cut 3⅜" x 40" strip(s):	1	4
2. Crosscut strip(s) into 3⅜" x 3⅜" squares:	10	40
3. Cut each square in half once diagonally to yield half-square triangles (C):	20	80
4. Cut 3" x 40" strip(s):	1	4
5. Crosscut strip(s) into		
3" x 5½" rectangles (D):	4	16
3" x 3" squares (E):	4	16
6. Cut 1¾" x 40" strip(s) (F):	1	3
7. For lap/twin, cut a 1¾" x 40" strip in half crosswise to yield, 1¾" x 20" strips (F):	—	2 (1 left over)
Fabric 3		
1. Cut 1¾" x 40" strips (F):	2	4
2. For lap/twin, cut 1 strip in half crosswise to yield, 1¾" x 20" strips (F):	—	2
Fabric 4		
1. Cut 5½" x 40" strip(s):	1	2
2. Crosscut strip(s) into 5½" x 5½" squares (G):	4	8
3. Cut 3⅜" x 40" strips:	2	4
4. Crosscut strip(s) into 3⅜" x 3⅜" squares:	16	38
5. Cut each square in half once diagonally to yield half-square triangles (C):	32	76
Fabric 5		
1. For lap/twin, cut 6¼" x 40" strip:	—	1
2. Crosscut strip into 6¼" x 6¼" squares:	—	2
3. Cut each square in half twice diagonally to yield quarter-square triangles (B):	—	8
4. For lap/twin, cut 5½" x 40" strips:	—	3
5. Crosscut into		
5½" x 13" rectangles (J):	—	4
5½" x 8" rectangles (I):	—	4
6. Cut 3" x 40" strip(s):	1	3
7. Crosscut into		
3" x 5½" rectangles (D):	4	8
3" x 3" squares (E):	4	12

CUTTING (continued)

All measurements include ¼"-wide seam allowances.

	Number to Cut	
	Crib/Wall Hanging	**Lap/Twin**
Fabric 5 (continued)		
8. Cut 1¾" x 40" strip(s) (F):	1	2
9. For lap/twin, cut 1 strip in half crosswise to yield 1¾" x 20" strips (F):	—	2 (1 left over)
Fabric 6		
1. Cut 8" x 40" strip:	1	1
2. Crosscut into 8" x 8" squares (M):	4	4
3. Cut 6½" x 40" strips:	2	4
4. For crib, crosscut into 5½" x 6½" rectangles (L):	8	—
For lap/twin, crosscut into 6½" x 18" rectangles (L):	—	8
5. Cut 6¼" x 40" strip:	1	1
6. Crosscut into 6¼" x 6¼" squares:	3	3
7. Cut each square in half twice diagonally to yield quarter-square triangles (B):	12	12
8. From the remainder of the strip, cut 4¹⁄₁₆" x 4¹⁄₁₆" square(s) (A)*:	1	4
9. Cut 3" x 40" strip:	1	1
10. Crosscut into 3" x 3" squares (E):	8	8
11. Cut 2" x 40" strip:	1	1
12. Crosscut into 2" x 2" squares (K):	16	16
Fabric 7		
For lap/twin, cut 4¹⁄₁₆" x 4¹⁄₁₆" square (A)*:	—	1
Binding fabric		
Cut 2½" x 40" strips:	4	7

To cut the 4¹⁄₁₆" measurements, cut halfway between 4" and 4⅛".

QUILT-TOP ASSEMBLY FOR LAP/TWIN SIZE

1. Using one 1¾" x 40" F strip each of fabrics 3 and 5, make one strip set. Repeat to make one strip set using one 1¾" x 20" F strip each of fabrics 3 and 5. From the strip sets, cut 24 segments, 1¾" wide.

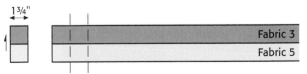

Make 1 full-length and 1 half-length strip set.
Cut 24 segments.

2. Make two strip sets using the 1¾" x 40" F strips of fabrics 2 and 3. Repeat to make one strip set using the 1¾" x 20" F strips of fabrics 2 and 3. From the strip sets, cut 48 segments, 1¾" wide.

Make 2 full-length and 1 half-length strip set.
Cut 48 segments.

3. Sew the segments from steps 1 and 2 together as shown to make four patch units. Make 12 using the fabric 2-3 segments and 24 using one fabric 3-5 segment and one fabric 2-3 segment.

Make 12.   Make 24.

4. Using the four-patch units and the E and D squares and rectangles of fabrics 2 and 5, assemble the Chain Square blocks as shown. Make the number indicated for each color combination.

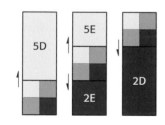

Make 8.

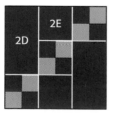

Make 4.

5. Using the B triangles of fabrics 1, 5, and 6 and the C triangles of fabrics 2 and 4, make flying geese units as shown. Make the number indicated for each color combination.

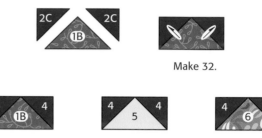

Make 32.

Make 16.   Make 8.   Make 12.

6. Sew the fabric flying-geese units with the fabric 1 center triangles together as shown to make the Flying Geese blocks. Make 16.

Make 16.

7. Using the A squares of fabrics 6 and 7 and the C triangles of fabrics 2 and 4, make the Square-in-a-Square blocks as shown. Make the number indicated for each color combination.

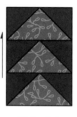

Make 1.   Make 4.

8. Sew the Flying Geese blocks to the Square-in-a-Square blocks as shown.

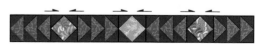

Make 1.

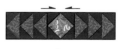

Make 2.

9. Sew the Chain Square blocks, the Flying Geese blocks, the flying-geese units, the G squares of fabric 4, and the E, I, and J pieces of fabric 5 together as shown to make the corner units. Make four.

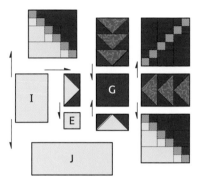

Make 4.

10. Sew the corner units to the strips from step 8 as shown.

QUILT-TOP ASSEMBLY FOR CRIB/WALL-HANGING SIZE

1. Refer to steps 1 and 2 of the lap/twin instructions to make one strip set using the 1¾" x 40" F strips of fabrics 3 and 5 and one strip set using the 1¾" x 40" F strips of fabrics 2 and 3. From each strip set, cut 12 segments, 1¾" wide.

2. Refer to step 3 of the lap/twin instructions to sew the segments from step 1 above together to make 12 four-patch units using one fabric 2-3 segment and one fabric 3-5 segment.

Make 12.

3. Refer to step 4 of the lap/twin instructions to make four Chain Square blocks using the four-patch units and the D rectangles and E squares of fabrics 2 and 5.

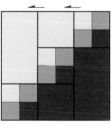

Make 4.

4. Refer to step 5 of the lap/twin instructions to make the flying-geese units using the B triangle of fabrics 1 and 6 and the C triangles of fabrics 2 and 4. Make the number indicated for each color combination.

Make 8.

Make 4.

Make 12.

ALTERNATE QUILT

CRIB/WALL-HANGING SIZE

SEDONA SUNRISE, by Laurie Shifrin, 35½" x 35½".
Machine quilted by Diane Roubal.
Warm and earthy colors in this striking wall hanging reflect the vitality found in nature. As you can see, the border design lends itself to directional prints. The combination of basic shapes and uncomplicated textures resembles designs found in the Southwest.

5. Refer to step 6 of the lap/twin instructions to sew the flying-geese units together to make the Flying Geese blocks. Make four.

6. Refer to step 7 of the lap/twin instructions to use the A square of fabric 6 and the C triangles of fabric 2 to make one Square-in-a-Square block.

Make 1.

7. Sew one Flying Geese block to the sides of the Square-in-a-Square block as shown.

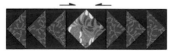

Make 1.

8. Sew the Chain Square blocks, the strip from step 7 above, and the Flying Geese blocks together as shown.

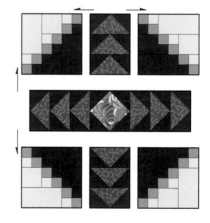

BORDER ASSEMBLY AND FINISHING

1. Sew the remaining fabric 4-6 flying-geese units to the G squares of fabric 4 and E squares of fabric 6 as shown to make the border star units. Make four.

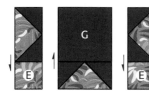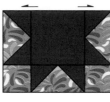

Make 4.

2. To make the inner-border strips, use a sharp pencil to draw a diagonal line on the wrong side of each K square. With right sides together, place a marked square on each end of each H strip as shown. Stitch on the marked line. Trim the seam allowance to ¼". Make eight.

Stitch.
Trim.

Make 8.

3. Sew each of the inner-border strips to an L outer-border rectangle as shown. Make eight. Sew a border unit to each side of the border star units as shown. Make four.

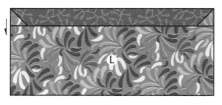

Make 8.

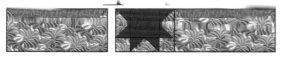

Make 4.

4. Stitch a border unit to each side of the quilt top. Stitch an M square to the ends of the remaining two border units. Sew these border strips to the top and bottom edges of the quilt top.

Lap/Twin
Quilt Assembly Diagram

Crib/Wall Hanging
Quilt Assembly Diagram

5. Refer to "Finishing" on pages 102–109 to layer the quilt top with batting and backing; baste. Quilt as desired. Bind the edges; add a label.

RED SKY AT NIGHT

By Laurie Shifrin, lap/twin size, 58" x 73". Machine quilted by Becky Kraus. Inspiration for this quilt came from the gorgeous red and black fern background batik. Its colors challenged me to create a striking two-color fabric variation of the Double Irish Chain pattern. The strong colors make a bold quilt with subtle shadings.

QUILT FACTS

	Crib	Lap/Twin	Double/Queen	King
Finished quilt size	48" x 58"	58" x 73"	83" x 98"	98" x 108"
Finished block size	7½" x 7½"	7½" x 7½"	7½" x 7½"	7½" x 7½"
No. of black Star blocks	1	2	6	9
No. of red Star blocks	4	6	12	16

MATERIALS

Yardage is based on 40"-wide fabric.

	Crib	Lap/Twin	Double/Queen	King
Red batik for blocks and chain squares	1⅛ yards	1⅜ yards	2⅜ yards	3 yards
Black batik for blocks and chain squares	1⅛ yards	1⅛ yards	2⅛ yards	2⅝ yards
Red-and-black print batik for background	2⅞ yards	4 yards	6 yards	8 yards
Backing	3¼ yards	3⅞ yards	7¾ yards	9¼ yards
Binding	⅝ yard	¾ yard	⅞ yard	1 yard
Batting	54" x 64"	64" x 79"	89" x 104"	104" x 114"

CUTTING

All measurements include ¼"-wide seam allowances.

	Number to Cut			
	Crib	Lap/Twin	Double/Queen	King
Red batik				
1. Cut 3¾" x 40" strip(s):	1	1	2	2
2. For crib and lap/twin, crosscut 3¾" x 40" strip into 3¾" x 3¾" squares (C):	4	6	—	—
• Trim remainder of 3¾"-wide strip to:	3⅜" wide	3⅜" wide	—	—
• For lap/twin size, crosscut 3⅜"-wide strip into 3⅜" x 3⅜" square:	—	1	—	—
• Cut 3⅜" square in half once diagonally to yield half-square triangles (B):	—	2	—	—
3. Cut 3⅜" x 40" strip(s):	1	1	3	3
4. Crosscut 3⅜" x 40" strip(s) into 3⅜" x 3⅜" squares:	8	11	24	32

CUTTING (continued)

All measurements include ¼"-wide seam allowances.

	Number to Cut			
	Crib	**Lap/Twin**	**Double/Queen**	**King**
Red batik (continued)				
5. Cut each square in half once diagonally to yield half-square triangles (B):	16	22	48	64
6. Cut 3" x 40" strips:	8	11	18	25
7. Crosscut 3" x 40" strips into 3" x 3" squares (A):	12	16	24	28
8. Set aside remaining strips for strip sets.				
Black batik				
1. Cut 3¾" x 40" strip:	1	1	1	1
2. Crosscut 3¾" x 40" strip into 3¾" x 3¾" square(s) (C):	1	2	6	9
3. From remainder of 3¾"-wide strip, cut 3⅜" x 3⅜" squares:	2	4	—	—
4. Cut each square in half once diagonally to yield half-square triangles (B):	4	8	—	—
5. From remainder of 3¾"-wide strip, cut 3" x 3" squares (A):	5	6	—	—
6. Cut 3⅜" x 40" strips:	—	—	2	2
7. Crosscut 3⅜" x 40" strips into 3⅜" x 3⅜" squares (B):	—	—	12	18
8. Cut 3" x 40" strips:	9	9	17	23
9. Crosscut 3" x 40" strips into 3" x 3" squares (A):	—	—	12	17
10. Set aside remaining strips for strip sets.				
Red-and-black-print batik				
1. Cut 8" x 40" strips:	2	2	4	6
2. Cut 5½" x 40" strip(s):	1	2	2	2
3. Crosscut 5½" x 40" strip(s) into 5½" x 13" rectangles (F):	2	4	6	6
4. Cut 3¾" x 40" strip(s):	1	1	2	3
5. Crosscut 3¾" x 40" strip into 3¾" x 3¾" squares (C):	5	8	6	9
6. Set aside remaining strips for quarter-square-triangle units.				
7. Cut 3" x 40" strips:	22	30	48	63

CUTTING (continued)

All measurements include ¼"-wide seam allowances.

	Number to Cut			
	Crib	**Lap/Twin**	**Double/Queen**	**King**
Red-and-black-print batik *(continued)*				
8. Crosscut 3" x 40" strips into				
3" x 23" rectangles (H):	4	6	10	12
3" x 15½" rectangles (G):	4	4	4	4
3" x 8" rectangles (E):	14	20	40	54
3" x 5½" rectangles (D):	4	4	4	4
3" x 3" squares (A):	20	32	72	100
9. Set aside remaining strips for strip sets.				
Binding fabric				
Cut 2½" x 40" strips:	6	8	10	11

QUILT-TOP ASSEMBLY

1. Using the 3" x 40" strips, make strip sets 1–6 as shown. Using 3"-wide red strips, 3"-wide black strips, and 8"-wide print strips, make strip sets 5 and 6 as shown. Refer to the chart on page 50 for the number of strip sets to make and the number of 3"-wide segments to cut from each strip set.

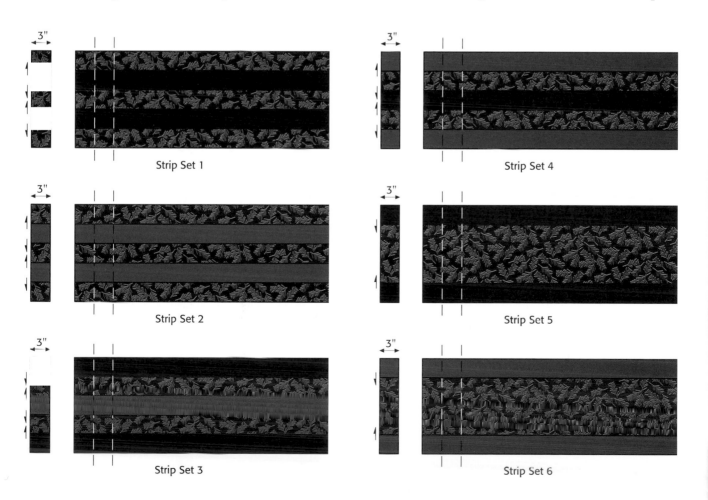

Strip Set 1

Strip Set 2

Strip Set 3

Strip Set 4

Strip Set 5

Strip Set 6

	Crib	Lap/Twin	Double/Queen	King
Strip Set 1				
No. of strip sets	2	2	3	4
No. of 3" segments to crosscut	14	20	39	52
Strip Set 2				
No. of strip sets	1	2	3	4
No. of 3" segments to crosscut	10	17	34	44
Strip Set 3				
No. of strip sets	1	1	2	2
No. of 3" segments to crosscut	4	8	18	24
Strip Set 4				
No. of strip sets	1	1	2	3
No. of 3" segments to crosscut	8	12	24	32
Strip Set 5				
No. of strip sets	1	1	2	3
No. of 3" segments to crosscut	8	12	24	32
Strip Set 6				
No. of strip sets	1	1	2	3
No. of 3" segments to crosscut	6	10	22	30

2. Refer to "Half-Square and Quarter-Square Triangles" on page 98 to use the red and print C squares (crib and lap/twin sizes) or the 3¾" x 40" strips (double/queen and king sizes) to make the number of quarter-square-triangle pairs shown in the "Number of Pairs" chart below. Repeat with the black and print C squares.

3. Sew each red quarter-square-triangle pair from step 3 to a red B triangle. Sew each black quarter-square-triangle pair from step 3 to a black B triangle.

Number of Pairs				
	Crib	Lap/Twin	Double/Queen	King
No. of red-and-print square pairs	4	6	—	—
No. of red-and-print strip pairs	—	—	2	2
No. of squares to mark and cut	—	—	12	16
No. of quarter-square-triangle pairs yielded	16	24	48	64
No. of black-and-print square pairs	1	2	6	9
No. of quarter-square-triangle pairs yielded	4	8	24	36

4. Arrange the red, black, and print A squares and the step 4 pieced squares to make the Star blocks. Refer to "Quilt Facts" on page 47 to make the number of red and black Star blocks indicated.

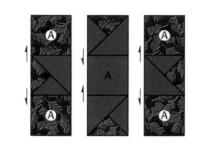

 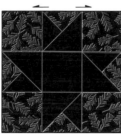

5. Sew a print E rectangle to the top and bottom of each Star block.

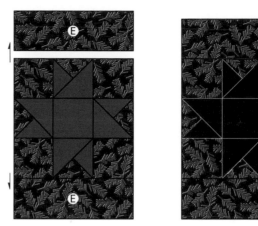

6. Stitch the red Star blocks and the strip set segments together as shown to make the red rows. Press seams toward the center of each red row. To make the black rows, sew the black Star blocks and the strip set segments together as shown. Stitch an F rectangle to the ends of each row. Press seams away from the center of each black row. Make the number of red and black rows indicated in the "Number of Rows" chart below.

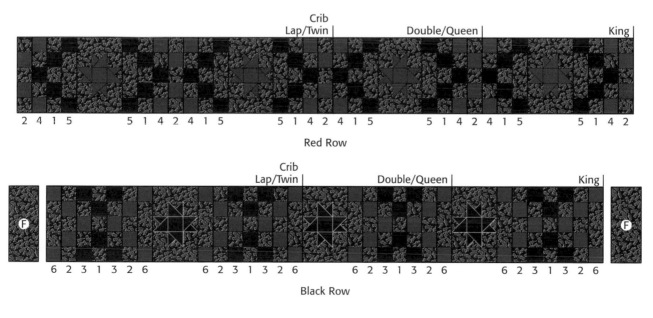

	Crib Lap/Twin		Double/Queen		King
2 4 1 5	5 1 4 2 4 1 5		5 1 4 2 4 1 5	5 1 4 2 4 1 5	5 1 4 2

Red Row

	Crib Lap/Twin		Double/Queen		King
6 2 3 1 3 2 6	6 2 3 1 3 2 6		6 2 3 1 3 2 6	6 2 3 1 3 2 6	

Black Row

Number of Rows

	Crib	Lap/Twin	Double/Queen	King
No. of red rows	2	3	4	4
No. of black row(s)	1	2	3	3

7. Beginning and ending with a red row, alternately stitch the red and black rows together.

   NOTE: *The lap/twin-size row assembly is shown.*

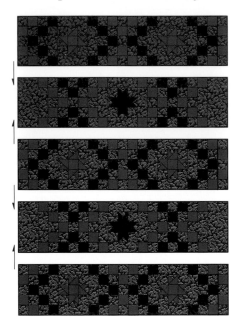

8. Beginning and ending with segments from strip set 1, alternately stitch segments from strip sets 1 and 6 together as shown. Sew a red A square and a print D rectangle to each end of the strip to make the inner top and bottom border strips. Make two.

   In the same manner, make the side borders by alternately stitching the red A squares and print H rectangles together as shown, beginning and ending with an A square. Stitch a print E rectangle to the ends of the strip. Make two.

   To make the outer top and bottom borders, stitch the black A squares and the print H rectangles together as shown. Stitch a G rectangle to the ends of the strip. Make two.

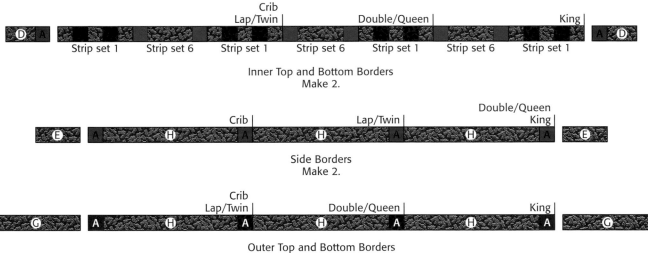

Crib
Lap/Twin | | Double/Queen | King |

D A   Strip set 1   Strip set 6   Strip set 1   Strip set 6   Strip set 1   Strip set 6   Strip set 1   A D

Inner Top and Bottom Borders
Make 2.

Crib | Lap/Twin | Double/Queen | King |

E   A   H   A   H   A   H   A   E

Side Borders
Make 2.

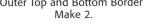

Crib
Lap/Twin | Double/Queen | King |

G   A   H   A   H   A   H   A   G

Outer Top and Bottom Borders
Make 2.

9. Refer to the quilt assembly diagrams on page 53 to stitch the inner top and bottom borders to the top and bottom of the quilt top. Stitch the side borders to the sides of the quilt top, and then stitch the outer top and bottom borders to the top and bottom edges of the quilt top. Press seams toward the borders after each addition.

10. Refer to "Finishing" on pages 102–109 to layer the quilt top with batting and backing; baste. Quilt as desired. Bind the edges and add a label.

ALTERNATE QUILT
CRIB SIZE

UNDERWATER ODYSSEY,
by Laurie Shifrin, 48" x 58".
Color variations of the multicolor batik give the
feeling of motion to this dark, brooding quilt.
Low-contrasting coordinating fabrics enhanced
by the quilting motifs give the feeling of being
in the depths of the ocean.

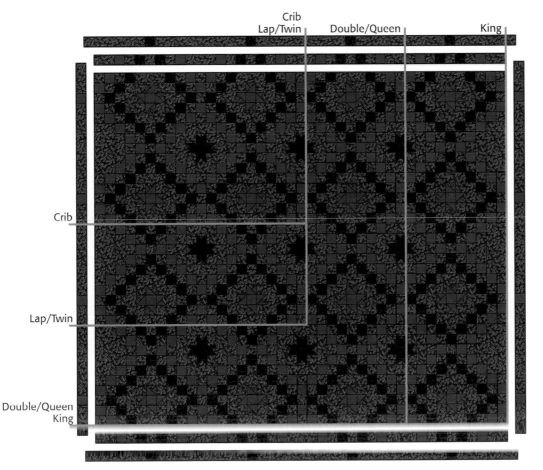

Crib
Lap/Twin   Double/Queen   King

Crib

Lap/Twin

Double/Queen
King

Quilt Assembly Diagram

MIXED UP BUT NOT CRAZY

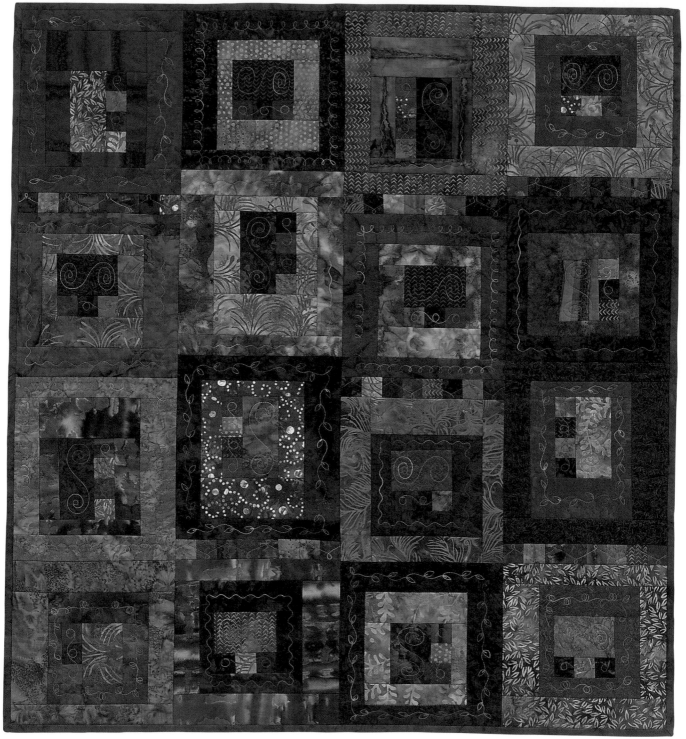

By Laurie Shifrin, crib/wall hanging size, 32½" x 35½". Machine quilted by Kathy Staley. Simple shapes and variations on just two blocks create this intriguing little quilt. The lopsided feel of the blocks is exaggerated by the placement of the small squares. This quilt is a great opportunity to use small cuts from your stash.

QUILT FACTS

	Crib/Wall Hanging	Lap/Twin	Double/Queen	King
Finished quilt size	32½" x 35½"	48½" x 70½"	80½" x 96½"	104½" x 113½"
Finished Square block size	8" x 8"	8" x 8"	8" x 8"	8" x 8"
No. of Square blocks	10	32	70	111
Finished Rectangle block size	8" x 9"	8" x 9"	8" x 9"	8" x 9"
No. of Rectangle blocks	6	16	40	58
Finished Chain block size	1" x 8"	1" x 8"	1" x 8"	1" x 8"
No. of Chain blocks	6	20	40	59

MATERIALS

Yardage is based on 40"-wide fabric.

	Crib/Wall Hanging	Lap/Twin	Double/Queen	King
12 or more coordinating batiks for blocks	⅜ yard *each*	¾ yard *each*	1½ yards *each*	2¼ yards *each*
Backing	1⅜ yards	3¼ yards	7¾ yards	9⅞ yards
Binding	½ yard	⅝ yard	⅞ yard	1⅛ yards
Batting	39" x 42"	55" x 77"	87" x 103"	111" x 120"

CUTTING

All measurements include ¼"-wide seam allowances.

NOTE: *Most strips need to be cut into smaller segments of varying widths. The segments decrease in size as you proceed through the cutting chart. Do not trim the width of the entire strip when the segment size changes.*

	Number to Cut			
	Crib/Wall Hanging	Lap/Twin	Double/Queen	King
Assorted batiks				
1. Cut 2½" x 40" strips:	10 *total*	32 *total*	70 *total*	111 *total*
2. From *each* 2½" x 40" strip, cut one				
2½" x 3½" rectangle (B):	10 *total*	32 *total*	70 *total*	111 *total*
2" x 5½" rectangle (F):	10 *total*	32 *total*	70 *total*	111 *total*
1¾" x 3½" rectangle (D):	10 *total*	32 *total*	70 *total*	111 *total*
1½" x 5½" rectangle (E):	10 *total*	32 *total*	70 *total*	111 *total*
1¼" x 3½" rectangle (C):	10 *total*	32 *total*	70 *total*	111 *total*
3. Cut 2¼" x 40" strips:	10 *total*	32 *total*	70 *total*	111 *total*

CUTTING (continued)

All measurements include ¼"-wide seam allowances.

	Number to Cut			
	Crib/Wall Hanging	Lap/Twin	Double/Queen	King
Assorted batiks *(continued)*				
4. From *each* 2¼" x 40" strip, cut one				
2¼" x 6" rectangle (H):	10 *total*	32 *total*	70 *total*	111 *total*
2¼" x 4½" rectangle (K):	6 *total*	16 *total*	40 *total*	58 *total*
2" x 8½" rectangle (I):	10 *total*	32 *total*	70 *total*	111 *total*
1¾" x 6" rectangle (G):	10 *total*	32 *total*	70 *total*	111 *total*
1½" x 8½" rectangle (J):	10 *total*	32 *total*	70 *total*	111 *total*
5. Cut 2½" x 40" strips:	6 *total*	16 *total*	40 *total*	58 *total*
6. From *each* 2½" x 40" strip, cut one				
2½" x 5½" rectangle (O):	6 *total*	16 *total*	40 *total*	58 *total*
1¾" x 4½" rectangle (M):	6 *total*	16 *total*	40 *total*	58 *total*
1½" x 4½" rectangle (L):	6 *total*	16 *total*	40 *total*	58 *total*
1¼" x 5½" rectangle (N):	6 *total*	16 *total*	40 *total*	58 *total*
7. Cut 2¼" x 40" strips:	6 *total*	16 *total*	40 *total*	58 *total*
8. From *each* 2¼" x 40" strip, cut one				
2¼" x 7¼" rectangle (P):	6 *total*	16 *total*	40 *total*	58 *total*
1¾" x 7¼" rectangle (Q):	6 *total*	16 *total*	40 *total*	58 *total*
1¾" x 8½" rectangle (S):	6 *total*	16 *total*	40 *total*	58 *total*
1½" x 8½" rectangle (R):	6 *total*	16 *total*	40 *total*	58 *total*
9. From the remainder of all the strips, cut				
1½" x 1½" squares (A):	102 *total*	320 *total*	690 *total*	1037 *total*
Binding fabric				
Cut 2½" x 40" strips:	4	7	10	12

NOTE: *Place same-size pieces into piles and label them with the appropriate letter to keep from making mistakes.*

QUILT-TOP ASSEMBLY

1. Using the A squares, stitch eight squares in random order as shown to make the Chain blocks. Sew four A squares together in random order as shown to make the segments for the Rectangle blocks. Sew three A squares together in random order as shown to make the segments for the Square blocks. Refer to "Quilt Facts" on page 55 to make the number of Chain blocks indicated. Make one Rectangle block segment for each Rectangle block indicated and one Square block segment for each Square block indicated.

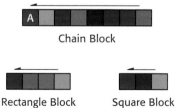

Chain Block

Rectangle Block Segment   Square Block Segment

2. To make the Square blocks, first sew a B rectangle to each of the Square block segments from step 1 as shown.

3. Select a C, D, E, and F rectangle that have all been cut from the same fabric. Stitch the C rectangle to one side of one unit from step 2 as shown. Stitch the D rectangle to the opposite side. Sew the E and F rectangles to the remaining two sides. Repeat for the remaining units from step 2.

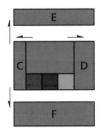

TIP

To give your blocks more variety, rotate the center units so that some are horizontal and some are vertical. You can also alternate the positions of the C and D rectangles and/or the E and F rectangles. This can also be done in step 4 but it is important that I and J are next to either E or F, and G and H are next to either C or D. (This can not be done with Rectangle blocks.)

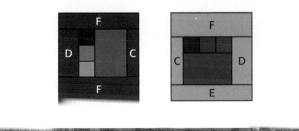

4. Select a G, H, I, and J rectangle that have all been cut from the same fabric but that are different from the rectangle fabric used in step 3. Stitch the G and H rectangles to opposite sides of one step 3 unit as shown. Sew the I and J rectangles to the remaining two sides of the unit. Repeat for the remaining units from step 3.

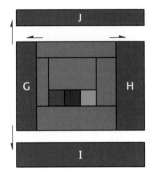

5. To make the Rectangle blocks, sew a K rectangle to each of the Rectangle block segments from step 1 as shown.

6. Select an L, M, N, and O rectangle that have all been cut from the same fabric. Stitch the L rectangle to one side of one unit from step 5 as shown. Stitch the M rectangle to the opposite side. Sew the N and O rectangles to the remaining two sides. Repeat for the remaining units from step 5.

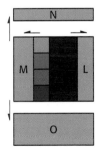

7. Select a P, Q, R, and S rectangle that have all been cut from the same fabric but that are different from the rectangle fabric used in step 6. Stitch the P and Q rectangles to opposite sides of one step 6 unit as shown. Sew the R and S rectangles to the remaining two sides of the unit. Repeat for the remaining units from step 6.

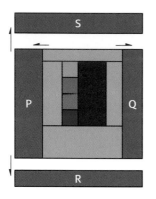

8. Refer to the quilt assembly diagrams on page 59 to arrange the Chain blocks, Square blocks, and Rectangle blocks in vertical rows. Within each vertical row (not horizontal row), you may alter the position of the blocks for a different layout. Sew the blocks in each vertical row together. In each row, press seams away from the Chain blocks. Press the remaining seams in opposite directions from row to row. Sew the rows together.

9. Refer to "Finishing" on pages 102–109 to layer the quilt top with batting and backing; baste. Quilt as desired. Bind the edges and add a label.

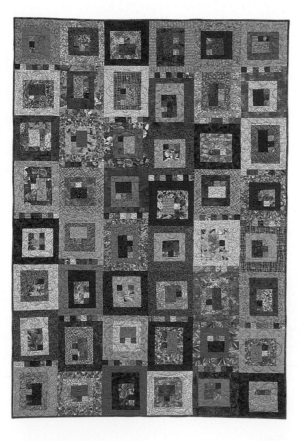

ALTERNATE QUILT

LAP/TWIN SIZE

SO, WHAT COLOR *IS* TEAL, EXACTLY?, by Laurie Shifrin, 48½" x 70½". Machine quilted by Becky Kraus. Teal is one of those colors that no one can really identify with a definitive example. This inspired me to use my collection of more than 40 teals, mixed with shades of plum and snowy white, to make this eye-catching quilt.

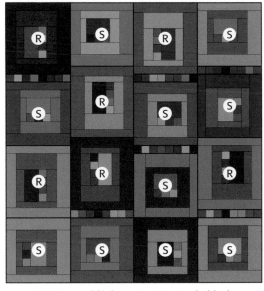

S = Square block   R = Rectangle block

Crib/Wall Hanging
Quilt Assembly Diagram

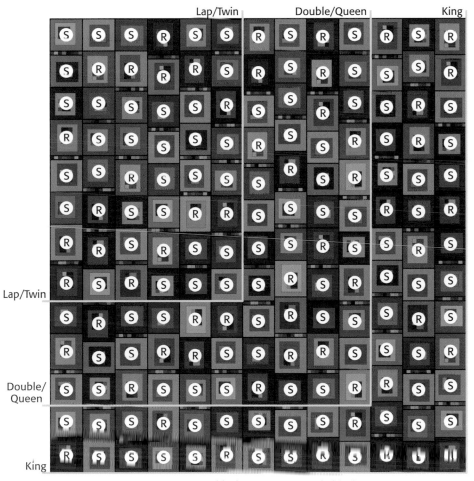

S = Square block   R = Rectangle block

Quilt Assembly Diagram

CIRCUS IN MY BACKYARD

By Laurie Shifrin, double size, 74½" x 74½". Machine quilted by Becky Kraus. The burst of color in this quilt was inspired by the vibrant border batik that is also used as the background. The subtle blue diamond formed by the block arrangement tricks the eye, and using four different fabrics for the inner border adds another interesting element to the quilt.

QUILT FACTS

	Lap/Twin	Double	Queen
Finished quilt size	54¾" x 54¾"	74½" x 74½"	94¾" x 94¾"

MATERIALS

Yardage is based on 40"-wide fabric.

	Lap/Twin	Double	Queen
Fabric 1: Blue batik for diamond squares	½ yard	¾ yard	1 yard
Fabrics 2–11: 10 coordinating batiks for remaining squares and inner border	½ yard *each*	¾ yard *each*	⅞ yard *each*
Multicolor print batik for background squares, outer border, and binding	2¾ yards	4¼ yards	5⅝ yards
Backing	3⅝ yards	4¾ yards	8⅞ yards
Batting	61" x 61"	81" x 81"	101" x 101"

CUTTING

All measurements include ¼"-wide seam allowances.

	Piece Dimensions		
	Lap/Twin	Double	Queen
Fabric 1			
1. For lap/twin and double, cut 4 strips:	2¼" x 40"	3" x 40"	—
For queen, cut 6 strips:	—	—	3¾" x 40"
2. Crosscut strips into 52 squares:	2¼" x 2¼"	3" x 3"	3¾" x 3¾"
3. Cut 1 square:	3" x 3"	3¾" x 3¾"	4½" x 4½"
4. Cut square in half once diagonally to yield 4 quarter-square triangles.			
Fabrics 2–11			
1. Cut 1 strip from *each* of fabrics 2–11:	3" x 40"	3¾" x 40"	4½" x 40
2. Crosscut each strip into 2 squares:	3" x 3"	3¾" x 3¾"	4½" x 4½"
3. Cut each square in half twice diagonally to yield 8 quarter-square triangles.			
4. For double, from the remainder of each strip, cut 5 squares:	—	3" x 3"	—
For queen, from the remainder of each strip, cut 1 square:	—	—	3¾" x 3¾"
5. For lap/twin and double, from *each* of fabrics 2–11, cut 2 strips:	2¼" x 40"	3" x 40"	—
For queen, from each of fabrics 2–11, cut 3 strips:	—	—	3¾" x 40
6. For lap/twin, crosscut into 31 squares*:	2¼" x 2¼"	—	—
For double, crosscut into 26 squares*:	—	3" x 3"	—
For queen, crosscut into 30 squares*:	—	—	3¾" x 3¾"

CUTTING (continued)

All measurements include ¼"-wide seam allowances.

	Piece Dimensions		
	Lap/Twin	Double	Queen
Fabric 2–11 (continued)			
7. From *each* of 4 of fabrics 2–11**, cut 2 strips:	1¾" x 40"	2" x 40"	2½" x 40"
Crosscut strips of **each fabric.*			
****Choose and cut the four fabrics after the center of the quilt top is completed so you can select the most effective colors for the inner border.*			
Multicolor print batik			
1. For lap/twin, cut 13 strips:	2¼" x 40"	—	—
For double, cut 17 strips:	—	3" x 40"	—
For queen, cut 22 strips:	—	—	3¾" x 40"
2. Crosscut into 216 squares:	2¼" x 2¼"	3" x 3"	3¾" x 3¾"
3. For queen, cut 5 strips:	—	—	2½" x 40"
4. From the remaining fabric, cut 4 strips:	6¼" x fabric length	7¼" x fabric length	8¼" x fabric length
5. For lap/twin and double, from the remaining fabric, cut 4 strips:	2½" x fabric length	2½" x fabric length	—
6. For queen, from the remaining fabric, cut 2 strips:	—	—	2½" x fabric length

QUILT-TOP ASSEMBLY

1. Cut a swatch from each of fabrics 1–11. Tape the swatches to a piece of paper; label each with its corresponding number. This will help you keep track of the fabrics in the next step.

2. Refer to the quilt assembly diagram on page 65 to arrange the background squares and fabric 1–11 squares as shown. Leave empty spaces where quarter-square-triangle units are indicated.

3. Look to see that you have an even distribution of colors and values throughout. Change the layout to provide a more pleasing arrangement if desired. You have extra squares of fabrics 2–11 if needed. Once you settle on an arrangement, sew the appropriate quarter-square triangles together to form squares as shown to fill the open spaces. You will need one quarter-square triangle from each of the four fabrics surrounding the open space. Place the squares so that each

quarter-square triangle is next to a square of the same color.

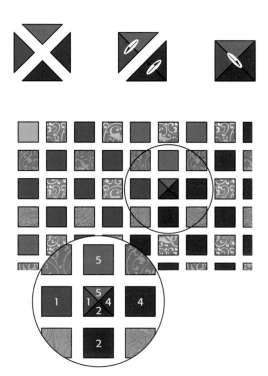

4. Sew the squares into vertical rows. Press seams away from the background squares, quarter-square-triangle units, and squares from fabric 1 that form the blue diamond. Sew the rows together. Press the seams in one direction.

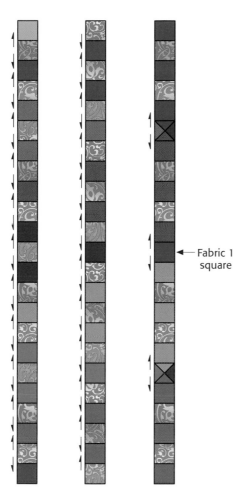

← Fabric 1 square

BORDER ASSEMBLY AND FINISHING

1. You can now decide which four fabrics you'd like to use for the inner border. Refer to "Cutting" on page 62 to cut two strips from each color. Sew the two strips of each color together so that you have one long strip of each color. Matching centers, sew an inner-border strip to each outer-border strip.

Make 4.

2. Measure the width of the quilt top through the center. On the wrong side of the quilt top, mark the middle of each edge with a sharp pencil or pin. Also mark ¼" in from each edge at the corners.

3. Divide the quilt-top width in half and subtract ¼" for the seam allowance. For example, if your quilt top measures 58":

$$58" \div 2" = 29"$$
$$29" - \frac{1}{4}" = 28\frac{3}{4}"$$

Fold each border strip in half to find the middle; mark the middle with a sharp pencil or a pin. Measure out in both directions from the middle point and mark the length you just calculated for the end marks (28¾").

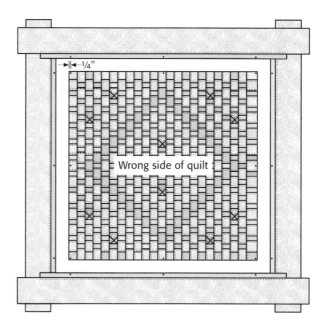

¼"

Wrong side of quilt

4. Pin a border strip to the quilt top, matching the middle and end marks. Pin every 3" to 4", easing in fullness if necessary. With the border strip on top, sew from one ¼" corner mark to the other, backstitching at each end. Repeat for the remaining border strips, being careful not to catch the previously sewn borders. Press the seams toward the borders.

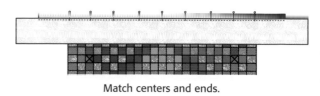

Match centers and ends.

5. To make the miter, fold the quilt top diagonally, right sides together, with the border edge toward you. Line up the border-strip seams and edges. Push the border seam allowance toward the center of the quilt top. Insert a pin along the border seam. Place a second pin in the excess border fabric and a third pin along the folded edge.

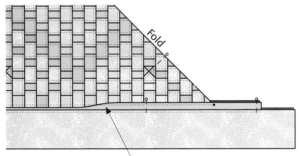

Push up the seam.

6. Place the ruler on the fabric so that the long edge is on the fold and the 45° line is on the border edge. Mark a line on the border strip with a pencil, starting where the stitching stops. Pin along this line, double-checking that the seams in the border strips are perfectly lined up.

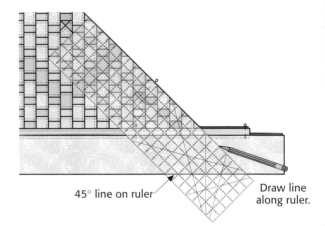

45° line on ruler

Draw line along ruler.

ALTERNATE QUILT
LAP/TWIN SIZE

CHINESE CHECKERS, by Laurie Shifrin, 54¾" x 54¾". Machine quilted by Kathy Staley. Vibrant colors against the dark floral print look like a colorful game board. The variation in values of blues, greens, and purples give this quilt a playful quality. Wouldn't it look great in solid Amish colors?

7. Backstitching over the first few stitches, sew on the marked line from the seam endpoint to the border edge. Rather than end this seam with a backstitch, which may distort the corner, reduce the stitch length over the last ½" of this seam.

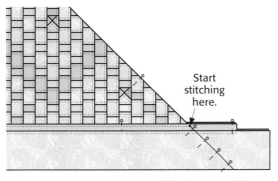

Start stitching here.

Pin along pencil line.

8. Remove all pins, open up the seam, and check to see if the mitered corner lies flat. Trim the seam allowance to ¼". Press the mitered seam to one side; press the seam allowance of the borders back down. Repeat to miter the remaining corners.

9. Refer to "Finishing" on pages 102–109 to layer the quilt top with batting and backing; baste. Quilt as desired. Bind the edges and add a label.

Quilt Assembly Diagram

ARBORETUM IN AUTUMN

By Laurie Shifrin, double/short queen size, 81" x 81". Machine quilted by Becky Kraus. The lush colors of the border batik are drawn out in the Circle-in-a-Square Log Cabin blocks. These might be colors you would see walking through a park in the height of a magnificent fall season.

QUILT FACTS

	Crib	Double/Short Queen	Long Queen
Finished quilt size	44½" x 44½"	81" x 81"	81" x 109⅝"
Finished block size	20¼" x 20¼"	20¼" x 20¼"	20¼" x 20¼"
No. of blocks	1	5	8

NOTE: *The inner-border detail makes this a slightly more complicated quilt. For a simpler version, just eliminate the piecing in the inner border.*

MATERIALS

Yardage is based on 40"-wide fabric.

	Crib	Double/Short Queen	Long Queen
Print batik(s) for log circle(s)	¼ yard	¼ yard *each* of 5 prints	¼ yard *each* of 8 prints
Solid batik for block chain squares	¼ yard	¼ yard *each* of 5 solids	¼ yard *each* of 8 solids
Solid batik(s) for block background(s)	⅝ yard	⅝ yard *each* of 5 solids	⅝ yard *each* of 8 solids
Solid batik for inner border	¾ yard	⅞ yard	1 yard
Solid batik for inner-border chain squares	¼ yard	¼ yard	¼ yard
Print batik for setting triangles and outer border	2 yards	3⅞ yards	5 yards
Backing	3⅛ yards	7⅝ yards	7⅝ yards
Binding	⅝ yard	⅞ yard	⅞ yard
Batting	51" x 51"	87" x 87"	87" x 116"

CUTTING

All measurements include ¼"-wide seam allowances.

	Number to Cut		
	Crib	**Double/Short Queen**	**Long Queen**
Print batik(s) for log circles			
1. Cut 2" x 40" strips:	2	2 *each* of 5 prints	2 *each* of 8 prints
2. Crosscut 2" x 40" strips into			
2" x 5" rectangles (C):	8	8 *each* of 5 prints	8 *each* of 8 prints
2" x 2¾" rectangles (B):	8	8 *each* of 5 prints	8 *each* of 8 prints
3. Cut 1¼" x 40" strip(s):	1	1 *each* of 5 prints	1 *each* of 8 prints
4. Crosscut 1¼" x 40" strip(s) into			
1¼" x 7¼" rectangles (D):	4	4 *each* of 5 prints	4 *each* of 8 prints
5. Set aside remainder of strip(s) for strip-pieced A squares.			

CUTTING (continued)

All measurements include ¼"-wide seam allowances.

		Number to Cut	
	Crib	**Double/Short Queen**	**Long Queen**
Solid batik(s) for block chain squares			
1. Cut 2" x 40" strip(s):	1	1 *each* of 5 solids	1 *each* of 8 solids
2. Crosscut 2" x 40" strips into			
2" x 2" squares (E):	8	8 *each* of 5 solids	8 *each* of 8 solids
3. Cut 1¼" x 40" strip(s):	1	1 *each* of 5 solids	1 *each* of 8 solids
4. Crosscut 1¼" x 40" strips into			
1¼" x 1¼" squares (A):	13	13 *each* of 5 solids	13 *each* of 8 solids
5. Set aside the remainder of the strip(s) for strip-pieced A squares.			
Solid batik(s) for block background(s)			
1. Cut 11" x 40" strip(s):	1	1 *each* of 5 solids	1 *each* of 8 solids
2. Crosscut 11" x 40" strips into			
11" x 11" square(s):	2	2 *each* of 5 solids	2 *each* of 8 solids
3. Cut each square in half once diagonally to yield half-square triangles (I):	4	4 *each* of 5 solids	4 *each* of 8 solids
4. Cut 1¼" x 40" strips:	3	3 *each* of 5 solids	3 *each* of 8 solids
5. Crosscut 1¼" x 40" strips into			
1¼" x 6½" rectangles (H):	8	8 *each* of 5 solids	8 *each* of 8 solids
1¼" x 4¼" rectangles (G):	8	8 *each* of 5 solids	8 *each* of 8 solids
1¼" x 2" rectangles (F):	8	8 *each* of 5 solids	8 *each* of 8 solids
Solid batik for inner border			
1. Cut 2⅝" x 40" strips:	2	5	7
2. For crib, crosscut strips into			
2⅝" x 18½" strips (L):	4	—	—
For double/short queen and long queen, stitch 2⅝" x 40" strips together to make 1 long strip.			
3. For double/short queen and long queen, cut pieced strip into			
2⅝" x 47" strips:	—	4 (L)	2 (M)
For long queen, cut remainder of pieced strip into			
2⅝" x 75½" strips:	—	—	2 (L)
4. Cut 2½" x 40" strips (K):	3	3	3
5. Cut one 2½" x 40" strip in half crosswise to yield two 2½" x 20" strips (K).			
6. Cut 2⅛" x 40" strip:	1	1	1
7. Crosscut 2⅛" x 40" strip into 2⅛" x 2⅛" squares:	16	16	16
8. Cut each square in half once diagonally to yield half-square triangles (J):	32	32	32

CUTTING (continued)

All measurements include ¼"-wide seam allowances.

	Crib	Number to Cut Double/Short Queen	Long Queen
Solid batik for inner-border chain squares			
1. Cut 2" x 4" strip:	1	1	1
2. Crosscut 2" x 4" strip into 2" x 2" squares (E):	4	4	4
3. Cut 1¼" x 40" strips (A):	2	2	2
4. Cut one 1¼" x 40" strip in half crosswise to yield two 1¼" x 20" strips (A).			
Print batik for setting triangles and outer border			
1. Cut 29⅞" x 40" strip(s):	—	1	2
2. Crosscut 29⅞" x 40" strip(s) into 29⅞" x 29⅞" square(s):	—	1	2

3. Cut each square in half twice
    diagonally to yield quarter-square
    side setting triangles:
	—	4	8 (2 left over)

4. Cut 15¼" x 40" strip:	1	1	1
5. Crosscut strip into 15¼" x 15¼" squares:	2	2	2

6. Cut each square in half once
    diagonally to yield half-square
    corner setting triangles.
	4	4	4

7. For crib, cut 6" x length of fabric strips:
    For double/short queen and long
      queen, cut 10" x remaining length
      of fabric strips:
	4
	
	—
		—
		
		4
			—
			
			4

Binding fabric			
Cut 2½" x 40" strips:	5	9	10

QUILT-TOP ASSEMBLY

1. Decide which log-circle, chain, and background fabrics will go together to make each block and place them in separate piles. Add the 1¼"-wide log-circle and block-chain strips you set aside in the cutting instructions to the appropriate piles.

2. Working with the fabrics chosen for one block, sew an A square to the ends of four F, G, and H

rectangles as shown. Stitch an E square to the ends of four B rectangles and four C rectangles.

Make 4 of each.

3. Sew the 1¼"-wide log-circle and block-chain strips into a strip set as shown. Crosscut the strip set into eight 1¼"-wide segments. Sew the segments together in pairs as shown to make four four-patch units.

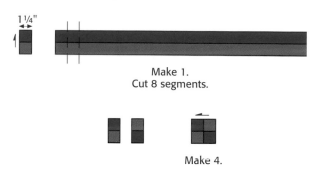

Make 1.
Cut 8 segments.

Make 4.

4. Sew an F rectangle to *each* four-patch unit, being careful to orient the four-patch unit correctly. Sew an A-F unit from step 2 to *each* four-patch unit. Make four.

Make 4.

5. Stitch a B rectangle and then a B-E unit from step 2 to each unit from step 4, followed by a G rectangle and an A-G unit from step 2. Then sew a C rectangle and C-E unit from step 2 as shown. Complete the unit by adding an H rectangle and an A-H unit from step 2 as shown. Make four complete log units.

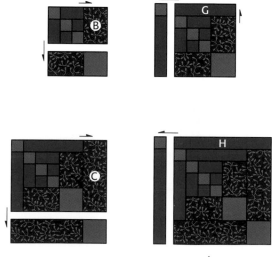

Make 4.

6. Sew a D rectangle between two log units as shown. Make two. Sew the remaining two D rectangles to each side of an A square as shown. Make one.

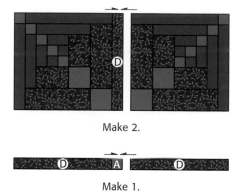

Make 2.

Make 1.

7. Stitch the units from step 6 together as shown.

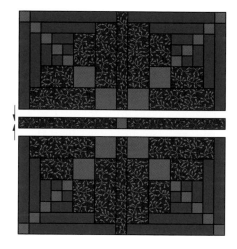

8. Sew matching I triangles to opposite sides of each unit from step 7. Add the remaining matching I triangles to the two remaining sides to complete the block.

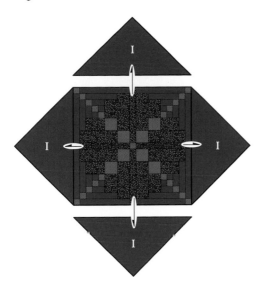

9. Repeat steps 2–8 to assemble any remaining blocks.

10. For the crib-size quilt, stitch a corner setting triangle to opposite sides of the block. Repeat for the remaining sides. For the double and queen-size quilts, refer to the quilt assembly diagrams to arrange the blocks and side setting triangles in diagonal rows as shown. Sew the blocks and triangles in each row together. Sew the rows together. Stitch a corner setting triangle to each corner of the quilt top.

Double/Short Queen Sizes

Crib Size

Long Queen Size

BORDER ASSEMBLING AND FINISHING

1. Sew a 2½" x 40" strip (K) of inner-border fabric to each side of a 1¼" x 40" strip (A) of inner-border-chain-square fabric. Repeat with the 20" strip lengths. From the strip sets, crosscut 40 segments, 1¼" wide.

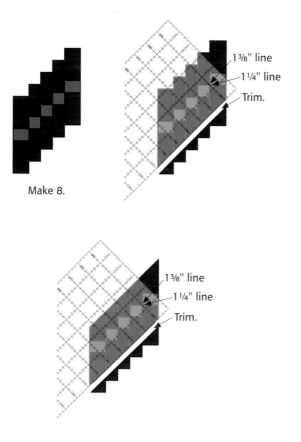

Make 1 full-length and 1 half-length strip set.
Cut 40 segments.

2. Sew five segments together as shown, matching seams. Make eight strips. Trim each strip to 2⅝" wide. To do this, center the points of the chain squares between the 1¼" and 1⅜" lines on a ruler. Trim. Rotate the strip and trim the opposite side in the same manner.

Make 8.

3. With right sides together, pin a J triangle to each end of each strip from step 2, extending the triangle edges slightly beyond the strip edges so that the edges will be aligned when the seam is pressed and the dog-ears trimmed; stitch. Press the seams toward the triangles. Trim the strip ends ¼" from the chain-square point as shown.

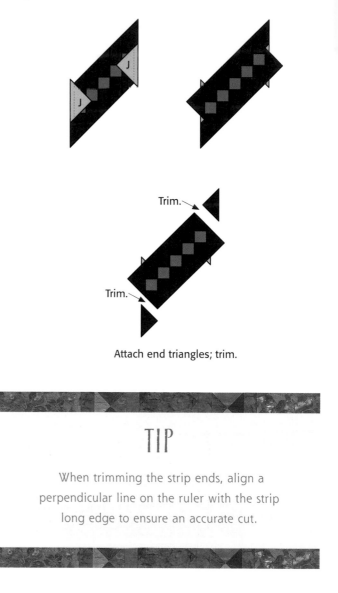

Attach end triangles; trim.

TIP

When trimming the strip ends, align a perpendicular line on the ruler with the strip long edge to ensure an accurate cut.

4. Sew a J triangle to opposite sides of each E square. Repeat for the remaining sides. Make four.

Make 4.

5. Refer to the quilt diagrams below to stitch a step 3 unit to each end of each L strip. For the long-queen size, also stitch a step 3 unit to each end of each M strip. Stitch an L strip to the sides of the quilt top. Stitch a step 4 square to the ends of the remaining two L or M strips. Stitch the strips to the top and bottom of the quilt top.

6. Refer to "Adding Borders" on page 101 to measure and trim the outer-border strips and sew them to the quilt top. It is very important to measure through the center of the quilt top, not at the edges, because there are bias edges in the pieced inner border.

7. Refer to "Finishing" on pages 102–109 to layer the quilt top with batting and backing; baste. Quilt as desired. Bind the edges and add a label.

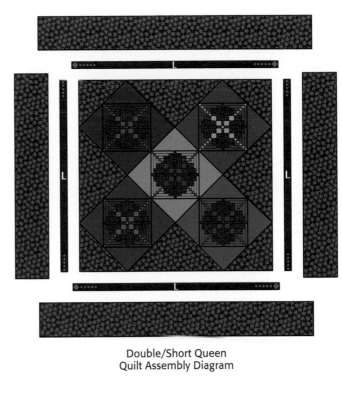

Double/Short Queen
Quilt Assembly Diagram

Crib
Quilt Assembly Diagram

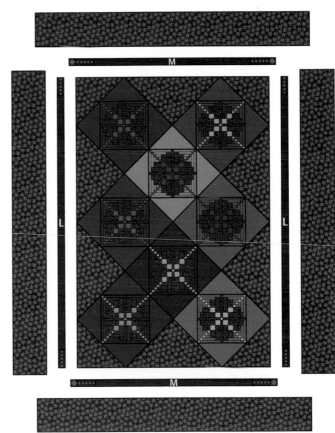

Long Queen
Quilt Assembly Diagram

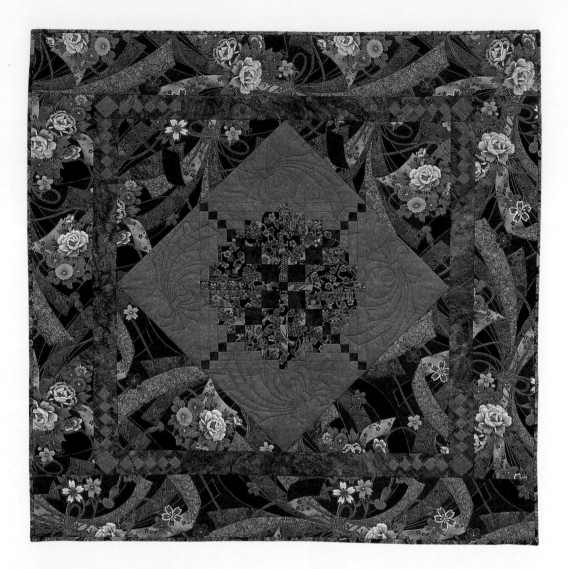

ALTERNATE QUILT

CRIB SIZE

NOSHI FOR LONG LIFE, by Laurie Shifrin, 44½" x 44½".
Machine quilted by Diane Roubal. A gorgeous, large-scale border fabric combined with batiks inspired this crib-sized quilt. The Japanese Noshi ribbon design is repeated in the quilting on the peach batik.

TWINKLE TOES

By Laurie Shifrin, twin/double size, 69½" x 81½". Machine quilted by Becky Kraus. My uncle Phil had a pet name for each of my three sisters and me; Twinkle Toes was mine. This quilt reminds me of the teasing that went on between us. Small triangles form pinwheels that twinkle against the chartreuse background batik. Notice the eye-catching triangles that are continued in the pieced border.

QUILT FACTS

	Crib/Lap	Twin/Double	Queen/King
Finished quilt size	54½" x 54½"	69½" x 81½"	99½" x 111½"
Finished block size	6" x 8"	6" x 8"	6" x 8"
No. of blocks	12	32	72

MATERIALS

Yardage is based on 40"-wide fabric.

	Crib/Lap	Twin/Double	Queen/King
Blue batik for blocks	⅜ yard	½ yard	⅞ yard
Purple batik for blocks	⅜ yard	⅝ yard	1⅛ yards
Dark green batik for blocks	⅜ yard	⅞ yard	1⅜ yards
Turquoise print batik for plain squares	⅜ yard	⅝ yard	⅞ yard
Chartreuse batik for background and middle border	1⅝ yards	3¼ yards	5⅞ yards
Animal-print batik for inner and outer borders	2¼ yards	3 yards	4¼ yards
Backing	3⅝ yards	5¼ yards	9⅜ yards
Binding	⅝ yard	¾ yard	1 yard
Batting	61" x 61"	76" x 88"	106" x 118"

CUTTING

All measurements include ¼"-wide seam allowances.

	Number to Cut		
	Crib/Lap	Twin/Double	Queen/King
Blue batik			
1. Cut 3¼" x 40" strip(s):	1	2 (D)	3 (D)
2. For crib/lap, crosscut 3¼" x 40" strip into 3¼" x 3¼" squares (D):	6	—	—
3. Cut 2½" x 40" strip(s):	1	2	5
4. Crosscut 2½" x 40" strips into 2½" x 2½" squares (A):	12	32	72
Purple batik			
1. Cut 3¼" x 40" strip(s):	1	2 (D)	3 (D)
2. For crib/lap, crosscut 3¼" x 40" strip into 3¼" x 3¼" squares (D):	6	—	—
3. Cut 2½" x 40" strips:	2	4	9
4. Crosscut 2½" x 40" strips into 2½" x 4½" rectangles (B):	12	32	72

CUTTING (continued)

All measurements include ¼"-wide seam allowances.

	Number to Cut		
	Crib/Lap	**Twin/Double**	**Queen/King**
Dark green batik			
1. Cut 3¼" x 40" strip(s):	1	2 (D)	3 (D)
2. For crib/lap, crosscut 3¼" x 40" strip into 3¼" x 3¼" squares (D):	6	—	—
3. Cut 2½" x 40" strips:	2	6	12
4. Crosscut 2½" x 40" strips into 2½" x 6½" rectangles (C):	12	32	72
Turquoise batik			
1. Cut 6½" x 40" strip(s):	1	2	3
2. Crosscut 6½" x 40" strip(s) into 6½" x 6½" squares (E):	4	7	17
Chartreuse batik			
1. Cut 8½" x 40" strip(s):	1	4	9
2. Crosscut 8½" x 40" strip(s) into 8½" x 8½" squares (F):	4	16	36
3. Cut 6½" x 40" strip(s):	1	2	3
4. Crosscut 6½" x 40" strips into 6½" x 6½" squares (E):	5	8	18
5. Cut 4¼" x 40" strips (G):	4	5	7
6. Cut 3¼" x 40" strips:	2	6 (D)	9 (D)
7. For crib/lap, crosscut 3¼" x 40" strips into 3¼" x 3¼" squares (D):	18	—	—
8. Cut 2½" x 40" strips:	3	6	14
9. Crosscut 2½" x 40" strips into 2½" x 4½" rectangles (B):	12	32	72
2½" x 2½" squares (A):	12	32	72
Animal-print batik			
1. Cut 4¼" x 40" strips (G):	4	5	7
2. Cut 5" x remaining length of fabric strips for outer border:	4	4	4
3. For queen/king, cut 3½" x 90½" strips from lengthwise grain for inner side borders*:	—	—	2
4. For queen/king, cut 3½" x 84½" strips from lengthwise grain for inner top and bottom borders*:	—	—	2

CUTTING (continued)

All measurements include ¼"-wide seam allowances.

		Number to Cut	
	Crib/Lap	**Twin/Double**	**Queen/King**
Animal-print batik (continued)			
5. For twin/double, cut 2½" x 62½" strips from lengthwise grain for inner side borders*:	—	2	—
6. For twin/double, cut 2½" x 54½" strips from lengthwise grain for inner top and bottom borders*:	—	2	—
7. For crib/lap, cut 3" x 39½" strips from crosswise grain for inner top and bottom borders*:	2	—	—
8. For crib/lap, cut 3" x 34½" strips from crosswise grain for inner side borders*:	2	—	—
The inner borders are cut to the exact lengths so that the pieced middle border will fit.			
Binding fabric			
Cut 2½" x 40" strips:	6	8	12

QUILT-TOP ASSEMBLY

1. **For the crib/lap size,** refer to "Quarter-Square-Triangle Units" on page 99 to pair each blue, purple, and green D square with a chartreuse D square; stitch and cut apart the quarter-square-triangle pairs.

   For the twin/double and queen/king sizes, refer to "Multiple Quarter-Square-Triangle Units" on page 100 to pair each blue, purple, and green D strip with a chartreuse D strip; mark the number of squares indicated in the "Units for Quilt Top" chart on page 79 *for each color combination.* Stitch and cut apart the quarter-square-triangle pairs.

   For all sizes, stitch two pieced triangles of the same colors together as shown to make a quarter-square-triangle unit. Make the number of units indicated for *each* color combination.

2. Stitch the A squares, the B rectangles, the C rectangles, and the quarter-square-triangle units from step 1 into strips as shown. Make one blue, green, and purple strip for each block in the quilt (refer to "Quilt Facts" on page 76).

   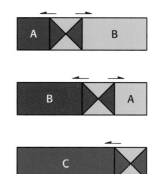

3. Stitch one of each strip from step 2 together as shown to complete the blocks.

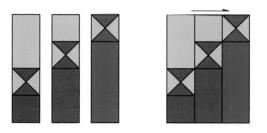

4. Referring to the quilt assembly diagrams on pages 80 and 81, arrange the blocks and the E and F squares into horizontal rows as shown, being careful to orient the blocks in the correct direction. Stitch the blocks and squares in each row together. Stitch the rows together.

NOTE: *The twin/double-size quilt arrangement is shown.*

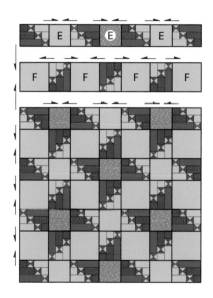

BORDER ASSEMBLY AND FINISHING

1. Using the chartreuse and animal-print G strips, refer to "Multiple Quarter-Square-Triangle Units" on page 100 and the "Units for Border" chart below to mark, stitch, and cut the number of squares indicated. Stitch two quarter-square-triangle pairs together to make a quarter-square-triangle unit. Make the number of units indicated.

2. Sew the quarter-square triangle units together as shown to make two middle side border strips and two middle top and bottom border strips.

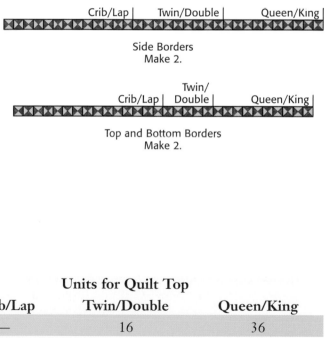

	Crib/Lap	Twin/Double	Queen/King

Side Borders
Make 2.

Top and Bottom Borders
Make 2.

	Units for Quilt Top		
	Crib/Lap	**Twin/Double**	**Queen/King**
No. of squares to mark	—	16	36
No. of quarter-square-triangle pairs yielded	24	64	144
No. of quarter-square-triangle units yielded	12	32	72

	Units for Border		
	Crib/Lap	**Twin/Double**	**Queen/King**
No. of squares to mark	28	42	62
No. of quarter-square-triangle pairs yielded	112	168	248
No. of quarter-square-triangle units yielded	56	84	124

3. Attach the inner side borders to the sides of the quilt top, pinning and easing if necessary. The quilt-top edges must fit the border strip exactly or the pieced middle-border strips will not align correctly. Attach the inner top and bottom borders to the top and bottom edges of the quilt top in the same manner.

Stitch the middle side border strips from step 2 to the sides of the quilt top. Stitch the middle top and bottom borders to the top and bottom edges of the quilt top.

Refer to "Adding Borders" on page 101 to measure and trim the outer-border strips and sew them to the quilt top.

4. Refer to "Finishing" on pages 102–109 to layer the quilt top with batting and backing; baste. Quilt as desired. Bind the edges and add a label.

Crib/Lap
Quilt Assembly Diagram

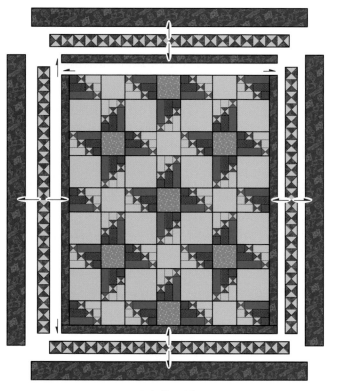

Twin/Double
Quilt Assembly Diagram

ALTERNATE QUILT

CRIB/LAP SIZE

WHIRLWIND, by Laurie Shifrin,
54½" x 54½".
The medium dark pinwheels contrast with the soft, undulating colors of the border fabric. Motion is created not only by the shapes but also by the subtle variation in values. The triangles of the inner border gently contrast with the border print.

Queen/King
Quilt Assembly Diagram

MURKY POND IN THE BERKSHIRES

By Laurie Shifrin, crib/lap size, 46½" x 53¾". Machine quilted by Becky Kraus. One of my favorite pastimes is driving along back roads, hoping to discover a hidden treasure at the end. One such road in Massachusetts led me to the most isolated, scummy pond that was rich with wildlife and intrigue. It became one of my favorite places to go to contemplate.

QUILT FACTS

	Crib/Lap	Twin	Double/Queen	King
Finished quilt size	46 ½" x 53¾"	61" x 75½"	82¾" x 90"	111¾" x 111¾"
Finished block size	7¼" x 7¼"	7¼" x 7¼"	7¼" x 7¼"	7¼" x 7¼"
No. of blocks	20	48	90	169

MATERIALS

Yardage is based on 40"-wide fabric.

	Crib/Lap	Twin	Double/Queen	King
At least 10 assorted batiks in light green, medium green, dark green, golds, and blues for blocks	⅜ yard *each*	⅝ yard *each*	⅞ yard *each*	1½ yards *each*
Coordinating polka-dot-print batik for inner border	½ yard	⅝ yard	¾ yard	⅞ yard
Dark green batik for mock piping middle border	⅜ yard	⅜ yard	½ yard	⅝ yard
Swirl-print batik for outer border and binding	1½ yards	2 yards	2½ yards	3½ yards
Backing	3⅛ yards	4⅞ yards	7¾ yards	10⅜ yards
Batting	53" x 60"	67" x 82"	89" x 96"	118" x 118"

CUTTING

All measurements include ¼"-wide seam allowances.

	Number to Cut			
	Crib/Lap	Twin	Double/Queen	King
Assorted batiks				
1. Cut 6⅜" x 6⅜" squares:	20 *total*	48 *total*	90 *total*	169 *total*
2. Cut each square in half twice diagonally to yield quarter-square triangles (C):	80 *total*	192 *total*	360 *total*	676 *total*
3. Cut 1 matching 6" x 6" square for every 6⅜" square:	20 *total*	48 *total*	90 *total*	169 *total*
4. Cut each square in half once diagonally to yield half-square triangles (B):	40 *total*	96 *total*	180 *total*	338 *total*
5. Cut 3½" x 3½" squares (A):	20 *total*	48 *total*	90 *total*	169 *total*
Polka-dot-print batik				
Cut 2½" x 40" strips:	4	6	8	10

CUTTING (continued)

All measurements include ¼"-wide seam allowances.

	Crib/Lap	Twin	Double/Queen	King
Number to Cut				
Dark green batik				
Cut 1½" x 40" strips:	4	6	8	10
Swirl-print batik				
1. Cut 7" x length of fabric strips:	4	4	4	4
2. Cut 2½" x length of fabric strips:	4	4	4	4

QUILT-TOP ASSEMBLY

1. Fold each A square in half, *wrong* sides to-gether; press along the fold to mark the center of opposite edges. Fold each B triangle in half along the long edge, *right* sides together; press approximately 1" along the fold, being careful not to stretch the fabric.

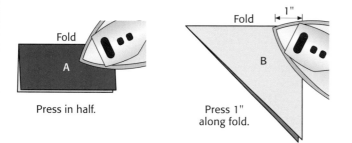

Press in half.   Press 1" along fold.

2. Select one A square, two B triangles of different fabrics, and two matching C triangles for each B triangle.

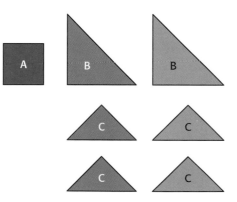

3. Sew the B triangles to opposite sides of the A square, matching center marks as shown. Line up the right edge of your ruler with the right edge of the square, the 1¾" line on the ruler aligned with the top and bottom triangle points, and one of the horizontal lines on the ruler with the seam line at the top of the square. Cut along the right edge of the ruler to trim away the excess triangle edges. Rotate the unit and repeat to trim the opposite edges of the triangles.

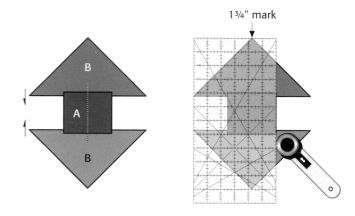

1¾" mark

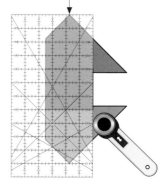

1¾" mark

4. Sew the C triangles together in pairs as shown, using one triangle of each color for each pair. Be sure the pairs are oriented correctly before sewing.

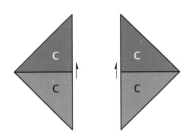

5. Sew the triangle units from step 4 to opposite sides of the step 3 unit as shown to complete the block.

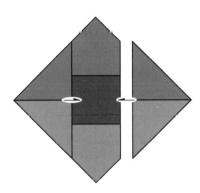

6. Refer to "Quilt Facts" on page 83 to repeat steps 2–5 to make the number of blocks required.

TIP

Mix and match the fabrics so that some blocks have similar colors or values and some have contrasting colors or values.

7. Refer to the quilt assembly diagram on page 86 to arrange the blocks in horizontal rows, rotating the blocks as desired to create an irregular look. Sew the blocks in each row together. Sew the rows together.

NOTE: *The crib-size arrangement is shown.*

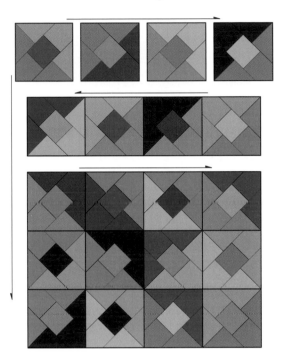

BORDER ASSEMBLY AND FINISHING

1. Refer to "Adding Borders" on page 101 to measure and trim the inner-border strips and sew them to the quilt top.

2. **For the crib-size quilt,** press all of the mock piping middle-border strips in half lengthwise, wrong sides together.

   For all other sizes, stitch the mock-piping middle-border strips together end to end to make one long strip. Then press the strip in half lengthwise, wrong sides together.

3. **For the crib-size quilt,** pin one strip to each side of the quilt top, aligning the raw edges of the piping and inner border; stitch. Press flat; *do not press the seam allowance to one side.* Trim the ends even with the quilt top. Repeat for the top and bottom edges.

   For the remaining sizes, align the raw edges of the one long piping strip with one side border strip; stitch. Press flat in the same manner as the crib-size quilt. Trim the ends even with the quilt top. Repeat for the remaining side and then the top and bottom edges.

   NOTE: *The crib-size quilt is shown.*

4. Refer to "Adding Borders" on page 101 to measure and trim the 7"-wide outer-border strips and sew them to the quilt top.

5. Refer to "Finishing" on pages 102–109 to layer the quilt top with batting and backing; baste. Quilt as desired. Bind the edges and add a label.

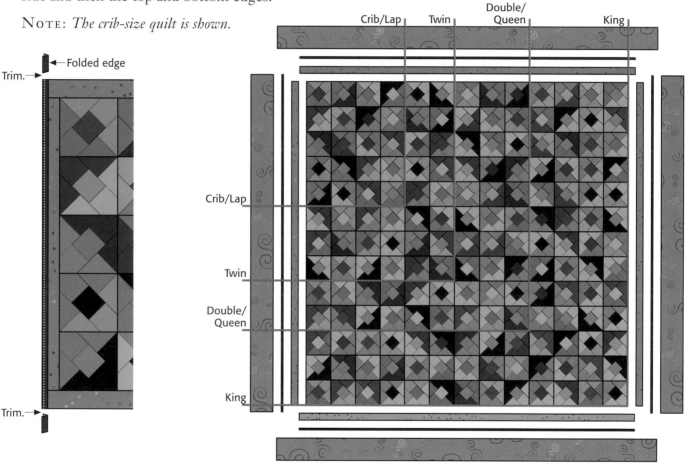

Quilt Assembly Diagram

ALTERNATE QUILT

Twin Size

SUNNY FIELDS, by Laurie Shifrin, 61" x 75½".
Machine quilted by Kathy Staley. Soft, hand-dyed pastel fabrics and flower prints are framed by a multicolored batik of the same colors. The diagonal element in the blocks, as well as the value differences of the fabrics, insures a quilt that offers something different every time you look.

PATCHWORK PUZZLE

By Laurie Shifrin, lap/twin size, 60½" x 72½". Machine quilted by Kathy Staley. Two simple blocks placed side by side create complex secondary and tertiary patterns. While the red and green squares form diagonal chains in one direction, the large stars and half-square red triangles give the illusion of a diagonal chain in the other direction.

QUILT FACTS

	Crib	Lap/Twin	Double/Queen	King
Finished quilt size	48½" x 48½"	60½" x 72½"	84½" x 96½"	108½" x 108½"
Finished block size	12" x 12"	12" x 12"	12" x 12"	12" x 12"
No. of Star blocks	5	10	21	32
No. of Chain blocks	4	10	21	32

MATERIALS

Yardage is based on 40"-wide fabric.

	Crib	Lap/Twin	Double/Queen	King
Fabric 1: Dark blue batik for blocks	½ yard	¾ yard	1¼ yards	1¾ yards
Fabric 2: Green batik for blocks	¼ yard	½ yard	⅞ yard	1 yard
Fabric 3: Dark pink print batik for blocks	⅜ yard	½ yard	⅞ yard	1¼ yards
Fabric 4: Brick red batik for blocks and border	⅜ yard	¾ yard	1⅛ yards	1½ yards
Fabric 5: Peach print batik for blocks	¼ yard	⅜ yard	¾ yard	⅞ yard
Fabric 6: Medium blue batik for blocks	⅜ yard	½ yard	1 yard	1⅜ yards
Fabric 7: Brown batik for blocks	¼ yard	⅜ yard	¾ yard	1 yard
Fabric 8: Green-and-peach batik for background	1 yard	1⅞ yards	3⅞ yards	5⅜ yards
Fabric 9: Multicolor dark print batik for border	1⅛ yards	1¾ yards	2¼ yards	2½ yards
Backing	3⅜ yards	4⅛ yards	8 yards	10⅛ yards
Binding	⅝ yard	¾ yard	⅞ yard	1 yard
Batting	55" x 55"	67" x 79"	91" x 103"	115" x 115"

NOTE: *Choose a background fabric that has color variations from area to area to add interest and dimension to your quilt.*

CUTTING

All measurements include ¼"-wide seam allowances.

	Crib	Lap/Twin	Double/Queen	King
			Number to Cut	
Fabric 1: Dark blue batik				
1. Cut 3⅞" x 40" strips:	2	4	9	13
2. Crosscut 3⅞" x 40" strips into				
3⅞" x 3⅞" squares:	20	40	84	128
3. Cut each square in half once diagonally				
to yield half-square triangles (A):	40	80	168	256
Fabric 2: Green batik				
Cut 2" x 40" strips (B):	2	4	10	14
Fabric 3: Dark pink print batik				
1. Cut 3½" x 40" strips:	1	2	4	6
2. Crosscut 3½" x 40" strips into				
3½" x 3½" squares (C):	10	20	42	64
3. Cut 2" x 40" strip(s) (B):	1	2	5	7
Fabric 4: Brick red batik				
1. Cut 2⅜" x 40" strip(s) (D):	1	2	3	4
2. Cut 2" x 40" strips (B):	3	6	12	17
Fabric 5: Peach print batik				
Cut 2" x 40" strips (B):	2	4	9	13
Fabric 6: Medium blue batik				
Cut 3⅞" x 40" strips (A):	2	3	7	10
Fabric 7: Brown batik				
Cut 3⅞" x 40" strip(s) (A):	1	2	5	7
Fabric 8: Green-and-peach batik				
1. Cut 7¼" x 40" strip(s):	1	2	5	7
2. Crosscut 7¼" x 40" strips into				
7¼" x 7¼" squares:	5	10	21	32
3. Cut each square in half twice				
diagonally to yield quarter-				
square triangles (E):	20	40	84	128
4. Cut 3⅞" x 40" strips (A):	3	5	12	17
5. Cut 3½" x 40" strip(s):	1	2	4	6
6. Crosscut 3½" x 40" strips into				
3½" x 3½" squares (C):	8	20	42	64
7. Cut 2⅜" x 40" strip(s) (D):	1	2	3	4
8. Cut 2" x 40" strips:	2	4	10	14

CUTTING (continued)

All measurements include ¼"-wide seam allowances.

	Number to Cut			
	Crib	Lap/Twin	Double/Queen	King
Fabric 8: Green-and-peach batik (*continued*)				
9. Crosscut 2" x 40" strips into				
2" x 2" squares (B).	20	40	84	128
10. Set aside remaining 2" strips for strip sets.				
Fabric 9: Multicolor dark print batik				
1. Cut 6½" x 40" strips:	4	6	8	9
2. Crosscut strips into				
6½" x 30½" rectangles (F):	2	1	1	—
6½" x 24½" rectangles (G):	2	1	1	—
6½" x 18½" rectangles (H):	—	6	10	14
6½" x 12½" rectangles (I):	2	2	2	4
6½" x 6½" squares (J):	2	1	1	2
3. Cut 3½" x 40" strip(s):	1	2	3	3
4. Crosscut 3½" x 40" strips into				
3½" x 3½" squares (C):	8	16	24	32
5. Cut 2" x 40" strip(s) (B):	1	2	3	4
Binding fabric				
Cut 2½" x 40" strips:	6	7	10	12

ALTERNATE QUILT

CRIB SIZE

GARDEN PARTY, by Laurie Shifrin, 48½" x 48½".
A lovely floral fabric with colors reminiscent of a garden in full bloom served as inspiration for this quilt. Because the values vary from the batik version, different elements of the design catch the eye. Notice the extension of the peach squares into the border.

QUILT-TOP ASSEMBLY

1. Referring to the "Four-Patch Units" chart below, sew the B strips into strip sets as shown. Crosscut the strip sets into the number of 2"-wide segments indicated for each. Stitch two segments from each strip together to make a four-patch unit. Make the number of four-patch units indicated.

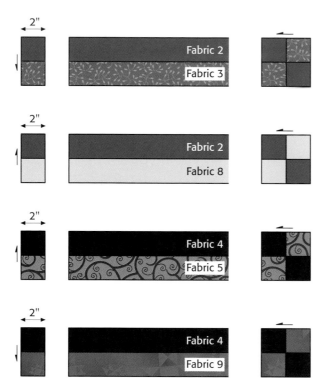

2. Sew each fabric 2-3 four-patch unit to a fabric 3 C square. Sew two of these units together as shown. Refer to "Quilt Facts" on page 89 to make one unit for each Star block in the quilt.

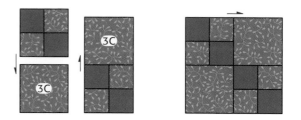

3. Sew the fabric 1 A triangles to each fabric 8 F. triangle as shown to make a flying-geese unit. Refer to "Quilt Facts" on page 89 to make four flying-geese units for each Star block in the quilt.

	Four-Patch Units			
	Crib	Lap/Twin	Double/Queen	King
No. of fabric 2 and 3 strip set(s)	1	2	5	7
No. of 2" segments to crosscut	20	40	84	128
No. of four-patch units	10	20	42	64
No. of fabric 2 and 8 strip set(s)	1	2	5	7
No. of 2" segments to crosscut	20	40	84	128
No. of four-patch units	10	20	42	64
No. of fabric 4 and 5 strip sets	2	4	9	13
No. of 2" segments to crosscut	32	80	168	256
No. of four-patch units	16	40	84	128
No. of fabric 4 and 9 strip set(s)	1	2	3	4
No. of 2" segments to crosscut	16	32	48	64
No. of four-patch units	8	16	24	32

4. Refer to "Multiple Half-Square-Triangle Units" on page 99 and the "Half-Square-Triangle Units" chart below to make half-square-triangle units from fabric 4 D strips and fabric 8 D strips. Sew each half-square-triangle unit to a fabric 8 B square as shown. Stitch the units together in pairs as shown.

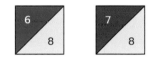

5. Refer to "Multiple Half-Square-Triangle Units" on page 99 and the "Half-Square-Triangle Units" chart below to make half-square-triangle units from the fabric 6 A strips and fabric 8 A strips. Repeat to make half-square-triangle units from the fabric 7 A strips and fabric 8 A strips.

6. To make each Star block, arrange two fabric 2-8 four-patch units from step 1, one unit from step 2, four flying-geese units from step 3, and two units from step 4 into vertical rows as shown. Sew the units in each row together. Sew the rows together. Refer to "Quilt Facts" on page 89 to make the number of Star blocks indicated.

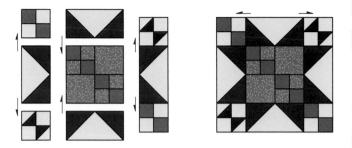

7. To make each Chain block, arrange four fabric 4-5 four-patch units from step 1, six fabric 6-8 and four fabric 7-8 half-square-triangle units from step 5, and two fabric 8 C squares together in vertical rows as shown. Sew the units in each row together. Sew the rows together. Refer to "Quilt Facts" on page 89 to make the number of Chain blocks indicated.

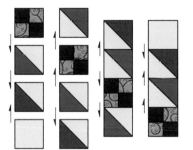
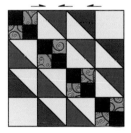

		Crib	Lap/Twin	Double/Queen	King
Half-Square-Triangle Units					
No. of fabric 4 and 8 strip pair(s)		1	2	3	4
No. of squares to mark		10	20	42	64
No. of half-square-triangle units					
yielded		20	40	84	128
No. of fabric 6 and 8 strip pair(s)		2	3	7	10
No. of squares to mark		12	30	63	96
No. of half-square-triangle units					
yielded		24	60	126	192
No. of fabric 7 and 8 strip pair(s)		1	2	5	7
No. of squares to mark		8	20	42	64
No. of half-square-triangle units					
yielded		16	40	84	128

8. Refer to the quilt assembly diagrams at right and on page 95 to arrange the blocks in horizontal rows as shown. Sew the blocks in each row together. Sew the rows together.

   NOTE: *The lap/twin-size quilt assembly is shown.*

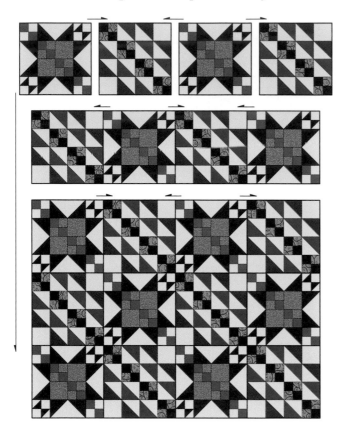

BORDER ASSEMBLY AND FINISHING

1. Sew each fabric 4-9 four-patch unit from step 1 of "Quilt-Top Assembly" to a fabric 9 C square. Stitch the units together in pairs as shown.

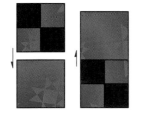 

2. Refer to the quilt assembly diagrams below and on page 95 to sew the remaining fabric 9 rectangles and the units from step 1 together to make the border strips. Stitch the side borders and then the top and bottom borders to the quilt top.

3. Refer to "Finishing" on pages 102–109 to layer the quilt top with batting and backing; baste. Quilt as desired. Bind the edges and add a label.

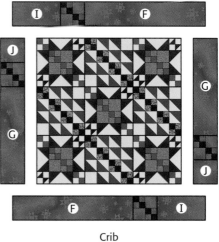

Crib
Quilt Assembly Diagram

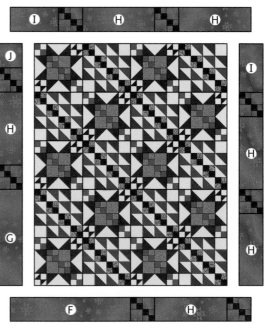

Lap/Twin
Quilt Assembly Diagram

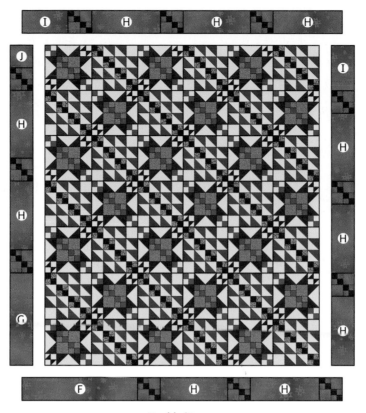

Double/Queen
Quilt Assembly Diagram

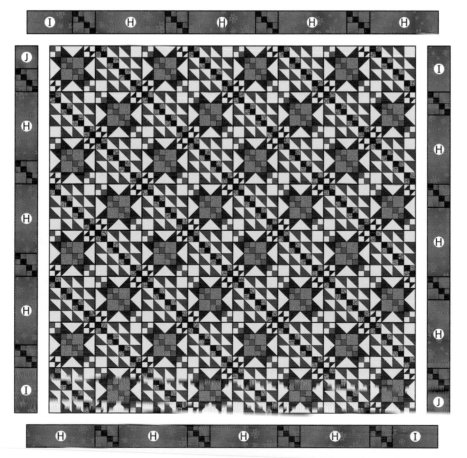

King
Quilt Assembly Diagram

BASIC QUILTMAKING TECHNIQUES

THIS SECTION INCLUDES general information about cutting and piecing your quilt. If you are a new quilter, these guidelines may offer ways to make your quilting experience easier. If you're an experienced quilter, these guidelines may just refresh your memory. I've also included some of my favorite tips for you to try. Instructions for finishing your quilt can be found beginning on page 102.

ROTARY CUTTING

THE BASIC rotary-cutting tools you'll need include a rotary cutter, an 18" x 24" rotary-cutting mat, and a 6" x 24" acrylic ruler. This size ruler will get you through all of the projects in this book.

Before you can rotary-cut the pieces needed for the quilt, you need to properly align the fabric. When you prewash fabric, the selvages shrink differently than the rest of the goods and tend to pucker and pull. To compensate for the distortion, fold the fabric in half lengthwise by bringing the two selvages together; then make a second fold by bringing the folded edge almost to the selvages. Now you can use the two folded edges for alignment and ignore the crooked selvages.

Place the folded fabric on the cutting mat with the raw edge to the right. Place the ruler on the fabric, near the right-hand raw edge, and align one of the horizontal grid lines of the ruler on the fold nearest you. Trim the uneven edge of the fabric

using the rotary cutter. Use even pressure on the blade and roll the cutter *away from you*, keeping it pressed against the ruler as you go.

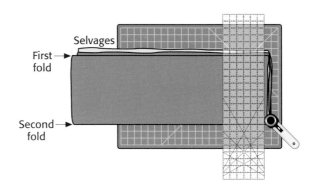

Rotate the mat and fabric 180° so that the clean-cut edge is on the left. (It may be necessary to fold the fabric on top of itself and pile it on the mat.) To cut a strip, line up the required measurement on the ruler with the clean-cut edge of the fabric. For example, if you want a 3"-wide strip, place the 3" ruler mark on the edge of the fabric. Remember to align a horizontal grid line on the ruler with the folded edge. Cut the strip. Cut all strips in this manner (from selvage to selvage) unless otherwise indicated. If the instructions specify a lengthwise cut, cut the strip(s) parallel to the selvage, aligning the selvage edges in the same manner as described previously for the cut edges.

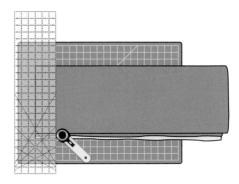

To cut a strip into pieces, place the strip horizontally on the mat, with one selvage to the right. Trim off the selvage or rough edge as you did when you trimmed the uneven edge of the whole fabric piece. Turn the mat around so that the clean-cut edge is on the left. Place the ruler so that a horizontal line is even with the long edge of the fabric and the desired vertical line is even with the left edge, and cut.

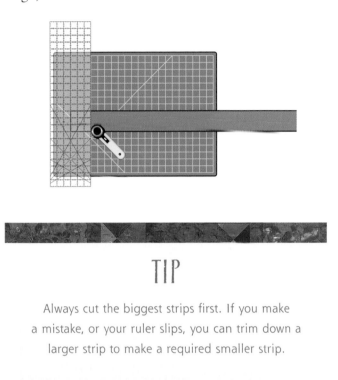

TIP

Always cut the biggest strips first. If you make a mistake, or your ruler slips, you can trim down a larger strip to make a required smaller strip.

MACHINE PIECING

THE MOST important aspect of machine piecing is to sew with an accurate ¼" seam allowance. If your seam allowance is off slightly, even by a few threads, your blocks may not fit together well and this will in turn affect other steps in the quilt-top assembly. I find that using a scant ¼" seam allowance (one or two threads of fabric less than ¼") makes up for the amount of fabric lost when pressing and gives me the most accurate ¼" seam allowance

Set your machine to stitch 10 to 12 stitches per inch. It is not necessary to backstitch at the beginning or end of seams.

TIP

Reduce your stitch length for the last ½" of all seams that extend to the outside edge of the quilt top. This will prevent the seams from opening when handled and will keep the outside edge measurement stable.

½"

Chain Piecing

Chain piecing is a machine-piecing method that lets you sew fabric pieces together quickly. To chain piece, sew the first pair of pieces from cut edge to cut edge. Stop sewing at the end of the seam, but do not cut the thread. Feed the next pair of pieces under the presser foot, about ¼" from the preceding pair. Continue feeding pieces through the machine without cutting the thread. When all the pieces are sewn, remove the chain from the machine and clip the threads between the pairs of sewn pieces.

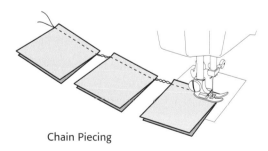

Chain Piecing

Easing

Occasionally, it becomes necessary to ease fabric when sewing two pieces together. This occurs when the edge of one piece is slightly longer than the other because of cutting discrepancies, seam width variations, or different fabric grains. To ease, pin the pieces together at the seams, ends, and in between, if necessary, to distribute excess fabric. With the shorter piece on top, stitch the seam. The feed dogs will ease the fullness of the longer piece, while the presser foot will lengthen the top piece.

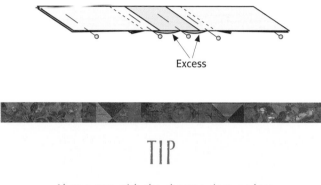

Excess

HALF-SQUARE AND QUARTER-SQUARE TRIANGLES

SEVERAL OF the quilts in this book are made with half-square and quarter-square triangles. The difference between the two is the position of the straight grain and bias grain. On half-square triangles, the straight grain is on the short sides of the triangle and the bias is on the long side. On quarter-square triangles, the straight grain is on the long side of the triangle and the bias is on the short sides. Follow the directions below for making half-square- and quarter-square-triangle units.

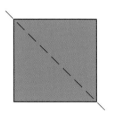 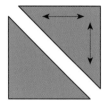

Half-square triangles

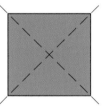 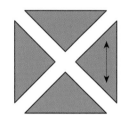

Quarter-square triangles

Half-Square-Triangle Units

1. Cut the squares the size specified in the cutting list. (This measurement equals the finished short side of the triangle plus ⅞".)

2. Pair squares right sides together, placing the lighter fabric on top. With a sharp pencil, mark a diagonal line from corner to corner on the wrong side of the lighter fabric. Sew a seam ¼" away from the diagonal line on each side.

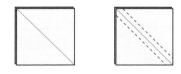

3. Cut on the marked line through both layers. Press the seams flat, and then press them toward the darker fabric. Trim the dog-ears. Each pair of squares will yield two half-square-triangle units.

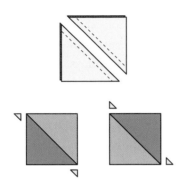

Quarter-Square-Triangle Units

1. Cut the squares the size specified in the cutting list. (This measurement equals the finished long edge of the triangle plus 1¼".)

2. Pair squares right sides together, placing the lighter fabric on top. With a sharp pencil, mark a diagonal line from corner to corner on the wrong side of the lighter fabric. Sew a seam ¼" away from the diagonal line on each side.

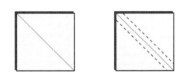

3. Cut on the *unmarked* diagonal. Then cut on the marked diagonal line. Press the seams flat, and then press them toward the darker fabric. Trim the dog-ears.

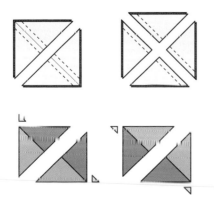

4. Use the quarter-square-triangle pairs as cut in step 3, or match two pairs together to form a quarter-square-triangle unit. For a scrappy look, mix up the pairs of fabric squares and then mix up the quarter-square-triangle pairs.

Quarter-Square-   Quarter-Square-
Triangle Pairs   Triangle Unit

Multiple Half-Square-Triangle Units

Use the following quick method when a pattern calls for multiple (more than ten) half-square-triangle units made from the same two fabrics. Cut the required number of strips of each fabric, but do not crosscut them into squares. Instead, follow these steps:

1. Place the strips right sides together, lighter fabric on top. With a sharp pencil, mark perpendicular lines to divide the lighter strip into segments the same size as the strip width. For example, if the strip is 2½" wide, mark lines at 2½" intervals.

2. Mark a diagonal line in each segment, forming a zigzag pattern across the squares. Sew ¼" on each side of the diagonal lines.

3. Rotary cut along the perpendicular segment lines and then along the diagonal lines. Press; then trim the dog-ears.

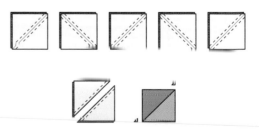

Multiple Quarter-Square-Triangle Units

The method for making multiple quarter-square-triangle units is similar to the half-square method described previously. Cut the required number of strips of each fabric. Follow steps 1 and 2 in "Multiple Half-Square-Triangle Units." For step 3, rotary cut along the perpendicular lines, but before cutting on the marked diagonal lines, cut each square in half on the opposite diagonal—the one without the marked line. Then cut on the marked diagonal to yield the quarter-square-triangle pairs. Each marked square will yield four quarter-square-triangle pairs. Press; then trim the dog-ears. Stitch two pairs together to make a quarter-square-triangle unit.

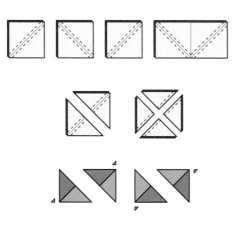

PRESSING

WHEN PRESSING, use a hot iron on the cotton setting. Pressing arrows are included in the diagrams when it is necessary to press the seams in a particular direction. When no arrows are indicated, the direction of the seam allowance doesn't matter.

In general, seams should be pressed in opposite directions wherever two seams meet. This technique, called butting, helps the fabric lie flat and gives a more accurate match, yielding perfect intersections. Press seams toward the darker fabric or toward the section with fewer seams, unless otherwise indicated. Press after each step.

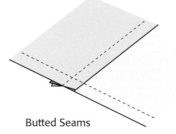

Butted Seams

TIP

For perfectly matched points, line up the pieces to be sewn, right sides together. Using your thumb and index finger, pinch just below the ¼" seam line where the points should line up. With your opposite hand, fold back the top piece where you are pinching to see if the points match; adjust if necessary, and then pin and stitch.

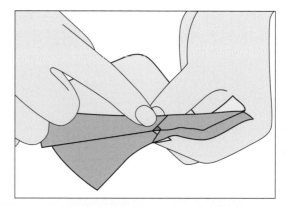

TIP

Lay the sewn piece to be pressed on an ironing board, with the seam positioned away from you and the fabric layer you want the seam pressed toward on top. Press the seam flat to set the thread into the fabric. If you have a cloth ironing board cover, this step will also make the fabric stick to it, which will keep your pieces from shifting while you're pressing. Separate the fabric layers. Place the iron on the right side of the bottom fabric and press the seam toward the top fabric, pressing away from you. Use the flattest part of the edge of the iron, not the tip, to push the layers apart, and be careful not to distort the shape.

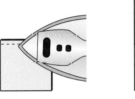 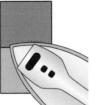

Overlap additional pieces about ½". You'll find that you need to iron for less time because the heat is retained in the stack of pieces.

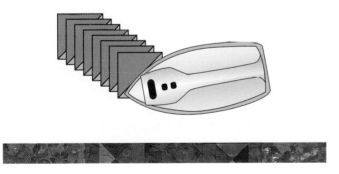

ADDING BORDERS

ALL OF the quilts in this book that are finished with borders use the straight-cut border technique, with the exception of "Circus in My Backyard" (page 60), which has mitered borders; instructions for mitering are given with that quilt.

Cut border strips on either the crosswise or the lengthwise grain as specified in the quilt instructions. Border strips cut on the lengthwise grain will be cut so that piecing is not necessary. Border strips cut on the crosswise grain will need to be pieced together end to end to make one long strip if the quilt edges are longer than the fabric width. After you cut the strips, and piece them together if necessary, cut the strips to the exact length using the following instructions.

1. Measure the length of the quilt top through the center from top to bottom. Cut two border strips to that length, piecing and trimming strips as necessary to achieve the required length. Mark the centers of the border strips and the sides of the quilt top.

2. With right sides together, pin the border strips to the sides of the quilt top, matching the center points and ends and easing as necessary. With the border strip on top, sew each border in place. Press the seams toward the border unless otherwise instructed.

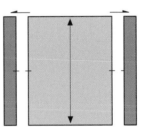

Measure center of
quilt, top to bottom.
Mark centers.

3. Measure the width of the quilt top through the center from side to side, including the borders you just added. Follow steps 1 and 2 to cut the border strips, mark and pin them, and sew them in place.

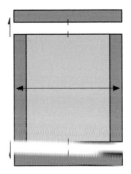

Measure center of quilt,
side to side, including borders.
Mark centers.

FINISHING

THE FOLLOWING PAGES include instructions for finishing your quilt, from choosing batting and piecing the backing to basting the quilting layers and adding a quilt label. You'll also find ideas on how to enhance your quilt with the quilting designs you choose—one more opportunity to be creative!

SELECTING BATTING

WHEN CHOOSING the batting for your quilt, consider your answers to the following questions:

- Will you be hand or machine quilting the project?

- Will you hang the quilt on a wall, or do you expect to use it?

- How drapey or poufed would you like the quilt to be?

Generally, the thinner the batting, the easier it is to hand quilt. You can choose either cotton or polyester; both are a pleasure to use. If hand quilting, avoid cotton battings that have a scrim—a thin mesh that the fibers are woven through. While a scrim helps stabilize the batting, it can be difficult to hand quilt. Heavily bonded polyester battings present a similar problem. The same bonded finish that prevents fibers from coming through the surface of the quilt can hamper hand quilting.

Thin to medium thicknesses of cotton, polyester, or cotton-and-polyester blend batting can be used for machine quilting. Thick polyester battings with lots of loft or pouf are used mostly for tied quilts. Cotton-and-polyester blends (usually 80% cotton and 20% polyester) are also popular with many quilters. They are easy to quilt, they give the look and feel of cotton batting, and the quilting stands out a bit more because the polyester fibers add a little loft.

If you want the quilt to "melt" or drape over the bed, use cotton batting. For wall-hangings, use a cotton or polyester batting that is not too thin; otherwise the quilt will not lie flat on the wall.

I recommend that you try as many battings as possible so that you are familiar enough with them to choose the right one for each project.

ASSEMBLING THE LAYERS

ONCE THE quilt top is complete, it is time to layer the top, batting, and backing. Cut your backing at least 4" larger than the top on all sides. Larger quilts may require a pieced back. It is acceptable to place the seams vertically or horizontally; choose whichever layout requires fewer seams and makes more economical use of the fabric. Trim all selvages before sewing the seams for the backing. Press the seams to one side for both hand and machine quilting.

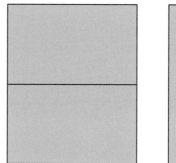

Horizontally Pieced Back

1 fabric width

Partial fabric width

Scrappy backings are another option. They can be fun when made from leftover fabrics from the quilt top. If you need only a few more inches of fabric, just add a strip of another fabric. This can create a quilt that is reversible. Be aware that the additional layers of fabric at every seam can make hand quilting more difficult.

Tape the backing, right side down, to a table or work surface large enough to fit the entire back. Begin by taping the middle of one side and then the middle of the opposite side, being careful not to stretch the fabric. Then tape the centers of the two remaining sides. Continue taping each edge from the middle out, about 6" apart, always working opposite sides.

Purchase a batting that is at least 3" larger than the quilt top on all sides. Carefully unfold the batting if it has been in a package. Because the batting fibers are not woven together, thin spots can be created if you pull too hard when unfolding. Place the batting over the backing. Smooth out any wrinkles by gently brushing your hands over the surface, working from the center out. Be careful not to stretch the batting. Trim any excess that is larger than the backing.

Place the well-pressed quilt top right side up over the batting, keeping the edges of the top parallel to the edges of the backing. Smooth from the center out, and along straight lines (like the inner borders or sashings) to ensure they remain straight.

If you are hand quilting, baste the layers together using quilting thread and a long needle. Work long running stitches from the center out, basting to each corner. Then baste a grid of horizontal and vertical lines 4" to 6" apart. Finally, baste around the perimeter of the quilt top, within ¼" of the edge.

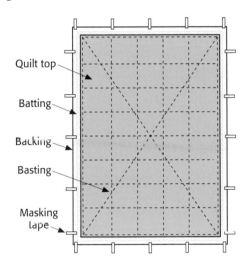

If you intend to machine quilt, use #2 rustproof safety pins to baste the layers together, placing the pins 4" to 6" apart. Try to avoid placing pins in areas you intend to quilt.

TIP

When thread basting the quilt layers, or the quilt "sandwich," use a teaspoon to help you lift the needle for an easier grip. You'll find this also helps lessen distortion of the quilt sandwich.

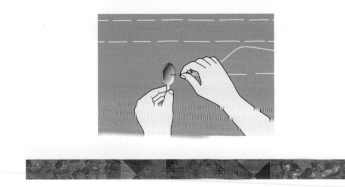

MARKING THE QUILT TOP

MARKING THE top is not always necessary. If you are stitching in the ditch or meandering in a random fashion, marking is not needed. More detailed quilt designs do need to be marked. With almost all marking tools, you can mark the quilt top after it has been basted into the quilt sandwich.

Use a marking tool that will be clearly visible on your fabrics. Always test the tool on a scrap of each fabric, to be sure the marks can be removed easily later on. For marking medium to dark fabrics, I like a chalk tool that dispenses powdered chalk in a thin line. These products are designed to wipe away after you're done quilting. For marking light fabrics, I prefer a water-soluble marker or pencil. Both make a visible line and are easy to use. There have been warnings that these products leave chemical residue on the fabric that may turn brown in the future. To prevent this from happening, rinse the entire quilt in clear water (no soap) when you are done quilting. This will remove the chemical from the batting and fabric.

To avoid having to wet the project after it is quilted to remove the quilting lines, use a silver pencil. Keep the tip very sharp and use a light touch; you can mark both light and dark fabrics. Silver marks are permanent but are the least visible of the pencil options.

QUILTING

WHEN DECIDING on your quilting designs, consider the desired effect. As a rule, the quilting should always enhance the quilt rather than distract the viewer. In most cases, batiks are so gorgeous, they speak for themselves and need little quilting enhancement. Other than securing the quilt sandwich, not much is required.

The most common kind of quilting, stitch in the ditch, neither adds nor detracts from the pieced design. It is done by stitching along the seams, on the side away from the seam allowance.

A nice way to add to the overall design of your quilt is to turn design elements from the fabrics into quilting motifs. Doing this helps maintain the character of the quilt and can expound on a theme. I find that curvilinear quilting images work well for a quilt that has lots of straight lines and angles, and straight-line quilting designs enhance appliqué quilts or quilts that give the illusion of curved patchwork.

The palm-frond batik used for the border of "Whirlwind" (page 81) inspired the quilting designs used throughout the quilt.

To decide how much quilting is needed, use the general rule that any unquilted space should be no bigger than your fist, or about 4" x 4". This will prevent sagging in large, unquilted areas and prevent excess stress on the fabric and quilting thread. Additionally, if the quilt is ever washed, you can be confident the batting will hold together.

Another basic guideline is that the quantity of quilting should be similar throughout the entire top. This ensures that the quilt will remain square and not get distorted after being quilted. A very common mistake is to quilt heavily toward the center of the quilt top in the patchwork area and do very little quilting in the border. This will surely lead to a wavy border!

Hand Quilting

To quilt by hand, use a quilting needle, quilting thread, and a thimble that fits securely on the middle finger of your dominant hand. Many quilters use a hoop or frame to support their work, but you can quilt without one provided your quilt has been well-basted. The following steps explain how to hand quilt. For more information on hand quilting, refer to *Loving Stitches: A Guide to Fine Hand Quilting* by Jeanna Kimball (That Patchwork Place, 2003).

1. Thread your needle with a single strand of quilting thread about 18" long. Make a small knot and insert the needle in the top layer about 1" from the place where you want to start stitching. Pull the needle out at the point where quilting will begin and gently pull the thread until the knot pops through the fabric and into the batting.

Quilted ribbons mimic the large-scale nonbatik print used in "Noshi for Long Life" (page 74).

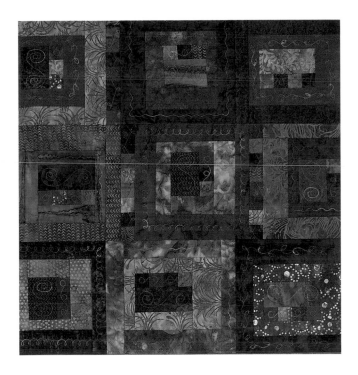

The square feeling of "Mixed Up but Not Crazy" (page 54) is enhanced by the curvy quilting lines.

TIP

Instead of trying to push the thread through the eye of the needle, it is easier to push the needle onto the thread. To do this, gently squeeze the thread end between the thumb and index finger of your nondominant hand. Recede the thread so it is covered by your fingers but you know where the end is. Push the eye end of the needle between your fingers and onto the thread. This method keeps the thread compacted and lessens the chance of it fraying at the tip.

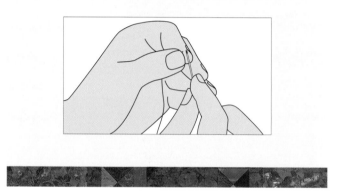

2. Take small, evenly spaced stitches through all three layers of the quilt. Place your other hand underneath the quilt so that you can feel the point of the needle with the tip of your first finger when a stitch is taken. Rock the needle up and down through all layers until you have three or four stitches on the needle.

3. To end a line of quilting, make a small knot close to the last stitch; then backstitch, running the thread a needle's length through the batting. Gently pull the thread until the knot pops into the batting; clip the thread at the quilt's surface.

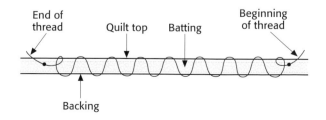

End of thread   Quilt top   Batting   Beginning of thread

Backing

TIP

If you aren't using a quilting frame and you can easily turn the area you are quilting upside down, then you can make both the starting and ending knots from the backside of the quilt.

Machine Quilting

Machine quilting lets you complete your projects quickly and is suitable for all types of quilts. For quilting straight lines, a walking foot is a must; it will let you feed quilt layers evenly through the machine without puckering. If your machine doesn't have a built-in walking foot, you will need a separate attachment.

For free-motion quilting, you will need a darning foot and the ability to drop the feed dogs on your machine. Guide the fabric under the needle in the direction of the design. This approach is very useful if you want to stitch over a design in a fabric or create curved patterns.

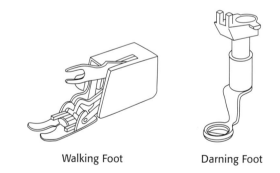

Walking Foot   Darning Foot

For more information on machine quilting, refer to *Machine Quilting Made Easy* by Maurine Noble (That Patchwork Place, 1994).

BINDING

AFTER YOU finish quilting your project, the final step is to bind the raw edges. I prefer double-fold binding for a fuller-looking, better-wearing edge.

You can cut the binding strips on the straight grain or on the bias. Bias will wear better and last longer on quilts that are handled frequently. Straight-grain binding will help make the edges of a wall hanging more square. The binding yardages in project instructions are for straight-grain strips; add an additional ⅛ yard to the measurements for bias binding.

For straight-grain double-fold binding, cut 2½"-wide strips from selvage to selvage. You need enough strips to go around the perimeter of the quilt top plus about 20" to allow for seams and finishing.

To cut bias binding strips, place the 45° line of the ruler along the edge of the fabric and trim off about 10" at one corner. Cut 2½"-wide strips parallel to the diagonal cut edge. When the edge becomes too long for the ruler, fold the fabric and align the cut edges as shown. Continue cutting until you have enough strips to go around the quilt top plus about 20".

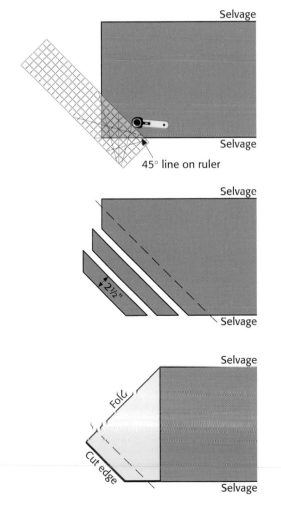

Attach the binding (straight grain or bias) as follows:

1. Join strips end to end with a diagonal seam. Trim the seam allowances to ¼". Press the seams open.

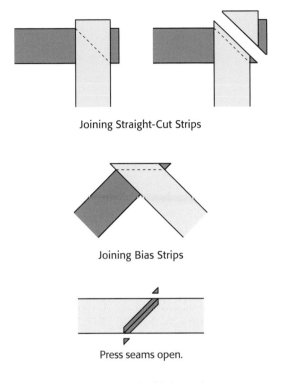

Joining Straight-Cut Strips

Joining Bias Strips

Press seams open.

2. Press the binding in half lengthwise, wrong sides together.

3. Set the machine for a slightly longer than normal stitch length (8 to 10 stitches per inch) and attach a walking foot. Starting near the middle of one side, align the raw edges of the binding with the edge of the quilt top. Leave a 6" tail of binding free. Stitch toward the corner with a ¼" seam. As you come near the corner, insert a pin ¼" from the lower edge. Sew up to the pin; backstitch.

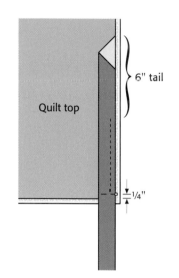

4. Without clipping the thread, take the needle out of the fabric, lift the presser foot and turn the quilt 90° counterclockwise, as if you are continuing on the next side. Fold the binding up and then down, even with the top edge. Start sewing again at the top edge. Repeat this process at each corner.

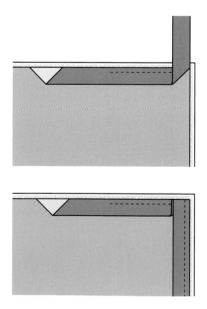

5. Stop sewing about 7" from where you began. Trim the start tail to about 1½" from where you stopped. Lay it flat on the quilt top. Overlap the end tail over the start tail. Trim the end tail so that the overlap measures 2½".

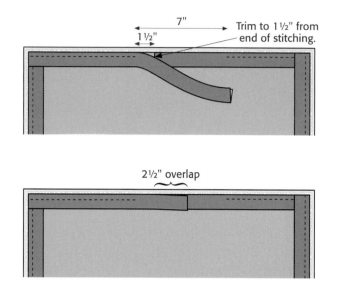

6. Open the start and end tails and place them right sides together at a right angle as shown. Secure with three pins. Mark the diagonal for a stitching line.

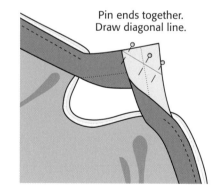

Pin ends together.
Draw diagonal line.

7. Stitch on the marked line. Check to make sure you've stitched correctly, and then trim the seam allowance to ¼". Finger-press the seam open. Refold the binding in half. Lay the binding flat along the edge and finish sewing the binding to the quilt top.

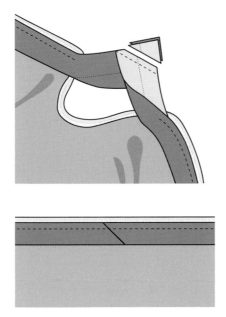

8. Trim the batting and backing slightly larger (about ⅛") than the quilt top—a good binding is full of batting. You may need to trim the batting and backing a little more or less depending on the thickness of the batting you use.

9. Fold the binding over the quilt edge to the back, making sure the binding covers the machine stitching. Using a blind hem stitch, hand stitch the binding to the backing; miter the corners.

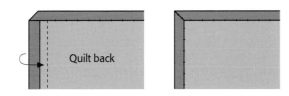

Quilt back

LABELS

PART of the pleasure of completing a quilt is adding a label to the back of the quilt. A label provides documentation of important information, including the name of the quilt, who made it, for whom or for what reason, when, and where. All who see the quilt in the years to come will treasure this information.

A label can be as simple or as elaborate as you want to make it. Use a permanent marking tool such as a Pigma Micron pen for hand writing. To keep the fabric from shifting as you write, tape it to your work surface or iron it to a piece of freezer paper. To help me keep my writing straight, I first draw lines on the freezer paper with a fat-tipped marker and then place the fabric over the line guide.

There are many new products available for printing your label using a computer. Ask for product information at your local quilt store, and follow your computer-printer manufacturer's instructions to make a computer-generated fabric label.

When the label is complete, press under the raw edges and attach it to the lower-right corner of the back of the quilt with a blind hem stitch.

RESOURCES

Visit the following companies' Web sites to see what new fabrics are available. Look for these fabrics, as well as those from Michael Miller Fabrics and Trans-Pacific Textiles, Inc., at your local quilt stores.

BATIK FABRICS

Bold Over Batiks!
www.boldoverbatiks.com

Hoffman California International Fabrics
www.hoffmanfabrics.com

Island Batik, Inc.
www.islandbatik.com

Marcus Brothers Textiles, Inc.
www.marcusbrothers.com

Princess Mirah/Bali Fabrications, Inc.
www.balifab.com

NONBATIK AND HAND-DYED FABRICS

Cherrywood Fabrics Inc.
www.cherrywoodfabrics.com

In The Beginning Fabrics
www.inthebeginningfabrics.com

Just Imagination
www.justimagination.com
www.judysfabric.com

Kona Bay Fabrics
www.konabay.com

Log Cabin Hand-Dyed Fabrics
Email: logcabindyes@cs.com

ABOUT THE AUTHOR

An avid seamstress since her teens and a quilter since 1980, Laurie Shifrin is now retail manager of In The Beginning, a fantastic quilt store in Seattle, Washington, where she lives. Laurie is also a quilting teacher, pattern tester, and most recently, quilt designer and technical editor for In The Beginning's latest book, *Playtime to Bedtime Quilts*.

Since the publication of her first book, *Batik Beauties*, Laurie's teaching and lecturing have taken her around the country, including an appearance on the television show *Simply Quilts* with Alex Anderson. If you're interested in seeing more of Laurie's published work, you can find her hand quilting in the cover quilt for the book *Threads From the '30s* (That Patchwork Place, 2000), which was compiled by Nancy J. Martin. And one of Laurie's original quilts is featured in Sandy Bonsib's book, *Quilting Your Memories* (That Patchwork Place, 2001).

new and bestselling titles from

America's Best-Loved Craft & Hobby Books®

America's Best-Loved Quilt Books®

NEW RELEASES
20 Decorated Baskets
Asian Elegance
Batiks and Beyond
Classic Knitted Vests
Clever Quilts Encore
Crocheted Socks!
Four Seasons of Quilts
Happy Endings
Judy Murrah's Jacket Jackpot
Knits for Children and Their Teddies
Loving Stitches
Meadowbrook Quilts
Once More around the Block
Pairing Up
Patchwork Memories
Pretty and Posh
Professional Machine Quilting
Purely Primitive
Shadow Appliqué
Snowflake Follies
Style at Large
Trashformations
World of Quilts, A

APPLIQUÉ
Appliquilt in the Cabin
Artful Album Quilts
Blossoms in Winter
Color-Blend Appliqué
Garden Party
Sunbonnet Sue All through the Year

HOLIDAY QUILTS & CRAFTS
Christmas Cats and Dogs
Christmas Delights
Creepy Crafty Halloween
Handcrafted Christmas, A
Hocus Pocus!
Make Room for Christmas Quilts
Snowman's Family Album Quilt, A
Welcome to the North Pole

LEARNING TO QUILT
101 Fabulous Rotary-Cut Quilts
Casual Quilter, The
Fat Quarter Quilts
More Fat Quarter Quilts
Quick Watercolor Quilts
Quilts from Aunt Amy
Simple Joys of Quilting, The
Your First Quilt Book (or it should be!)

PAPER PIECING
40 Bright and Bold Paper-Pieced Blocks
50 Fabulous Paper-Pieced Stars
Down in the Valley
Easy Machine Paper Piecing
For the Birds
It's Raining Cats and Dogs
Papers for Foundation Piecing
Quilter's Ark, A
Show Me How to Paper Piece
Traditional Quilts to Paper Piece

QUILTS FOR BABIES & CHILDREN
Easy Paper-Pieced Baby Quilts
Even More Quilts for Baby
More Quilts for Baby
Play Quilts
Quilts for Baby
Sweet and Simple Baby Quilts

ROTARY CUTTING/SPEED PIECING
101 Fabulous Rotary-Cut Quilts
365 Quilt Blocks a Year Perpetual Calendar
1000 Great Quilt Blocks
Around the Block Again
Around the Block with Judy Hopkins
Cutting Corners
Log Cabin Fever
Pairing Up
Strips and Strings
Triangle-Free Quilts
Triangle Tricks

SCRAP QUILTS
Nickel Quilts
Rich Traditions
Scrap Frenzy
Spectacular Scraps
Successful Scrap Quilts

TOPICS IN QUILTMAKING
Americana Quilts
Bed and Breakfast Quilts
Bright Quilts from Down Under
Creative Machine Stitching
Everyday Embellishments
Fabulous Quilts from Favorite Patterns
Folk Art Friends
Handprint Quilts
Just Can't Cut It!
Quilter's Home: Winter, The
Split-Diamond Dazzlers
Time to Quilt

CRAFTS
300 Papermaking Recipes
ABCs of Making Teddy Bears, The
Blissful Bath, The
Creating with Paint
Handcrafted Frames
Handcrafted Garden Accents
Painted Whimsies
Pretty and Posh
Sassy Cats
Stamp in Color

KNITTING & CROCHET
365 Knitting Stitches a Year
    Perpetual Calendar
Basically Brilliant Knits
Crochet for Tots
Crocheted Aran Sweaters
Knitted Sweaters for Every Season
Knitted Throws and More
Knitter's Template, A
Knitting with Novelty Yarns
More Paintbox Knits
Simply Beautiful Sweaters for Men
Today's Crochet
Too Cute! Cotton Knits for Toddlers
Treasury of Rowan Knits, A
Ultimate Knitter's Guide, The